HIGHLY EXALTED!

Studies In The Ascension Of Christ

Ken Chant

HIGHLY EXALTED!

Studies In The Ascension Of Christ

By Ken Chant

Copyright © 2012 By Ken Chant.

ISBN 978-1-61529-071-0

Vision Publishing
1672 Main Street E 109
Ramona, CA 92065
1-800-9-VISION
www.booksbyvision.com

A NOTE ON GENDER

It is unfortunate that the English language does not contain an adequate generic pronoun (especially in the singular number) that includes without bias both male and female. So *"he, him, his, man, mankind,"* with their plurals, must do the work for both sexes. Accordingly, wherever it is appropriate to do so in the following pages, please include the feminine gender in the masculine, and vice versa.

FOOTNOTES

A work once fully referenced will thereafter be noted either by "ibid" or "op. cit."

Contents

ABBREVIATIONS

Abbreviations commonly used for the books of the Bible are

Genesis	Ge	Habakkuk	Hb
Exodus	Ex	Zephaniah	Zp
Leviticus	Le	Haggai	Hg
Numbers	Nu	Zechariah	Zc
Deuteronomy	De	Malachi	Mal
Joshua	Js		
Judges	Jg		
Ruth	Ru	Matthew	Mt
1 Samuel	1 Sa	Mark	Mk
2 Samuel	2 Sa	Luke	Lu
1 Kings	1 Kg	John	Jn
2 Kings	2 Kg	Acts	Ac
1 Chronicles	1 Ch	Romans	Ro
2 Chronicles	2 Ch	1 Corinthians	1 Co
Ezra	Ezr	2 Corinthians	2 Co
Nehemiah	Ne	Galatians	Ga
Esther	Es	Ephesians	Ep
Job	Jb	Philippians	Ph
Psalm	Ps	Colossians	Cl
Proverbs	Pr	1 Thessalonians	1 Th
Ecclesiastes	Ec	2 Thessalonians	2 Th
Song of Songs	Ca *	1 Timothy	1 Ti
Isaiah	Is	2 Timothy	2 Ti
Jeremiah	Je	Titus	Tit
Lamentations	La	Philemon	Phm
Ezekiel	Ez	Hebrews	He
Daniel	Da	James	Ja
Hosea	Ho	1 Peter	1 Pe
Joel	Jl	2 Peter	2 Pe
Amos	Am	1 John	1 Jn
Obadiah	Ob	2 John	2 Jn
Jonah	Jo	3 John	3 Jn
Micah	Mi	Jude	Ju
Nahum	Na	Revelation	Re

Ca is an abbreviation of *Canticles*, a derivative of the Latin name of the *Song of Solomon*, which is sometimes also called the *Song of Songs*.

DISCOVERING TRUTH

"The truth of the faith,[9] said St Thomas Aquinas, "is diffused throughout Holy Scripture in various ways, and sometimes obscurely. Hence to bring out the truth of the faith from Holy Scripture requires long study and training. But not everyone who needs to know the truth of the faith can devote themselves to study. So a clear summary is needed of the truth set forth in Holy Scripture, so that everyone has the opportunity to believe it. This summary is not an addition to Holy Scripture; rather, it is drawn from Holy Scripture." [1]

I could say much the same about this book. Its writing cost me far more time and toil than most of my readers could afford, so in this I hope I have done you good service. It also consists in the main of a commentary on a substantial part of the anonymous *Letter to the Hebrews*. It is not however, a full commentary. You will find nothing here about date of composition, nor place, nor author, nor background material. If you wish to know those things, you will have to consult a regular commentary. I am interested here only in those parts of *Hebrews* that deal with the high priestly ministry of Christ.

The Saviour's heavenly priesthood is itself a product of the great event that climaxed his passion; that is, his ascension into heaven and his resumption of his seat at the right hand of the Father. The first three chapters of the book deal with the ascension; the remainder with his role as priest.

The end result, I trust, will be an answer to the question: where do you find true religion? There are four possible choices:

- you can search for it in rites and ceremonies, supposing that by observance of the proper rituals you will gain acceptance with God
- you can trust in some good work or personal sacrifice to purchase divine pardon and entrance into heaven
- you can repose confidence in holding correct opinions, learning orthodox doctrine and refusing to deviate from it

---

[1] Quoted in <u>Christian Classics</u>; ed. Veronica Zundel; Eerdmans Pub. Co., 1983; pg. 32; quoting from the "Summa Theologica" tr. by Mary T. Clark.

- or you can (as the author of *Hebrews* would) utterly reject such delusions and place your dependence wholly upon Christ, trusting only in his sacrifice and intercession.

In a word, that means holding to Christ as priest, the sole Mediator between heaven and earth. Trust in Christ leads to a work of grace that certainly occurs *in* us, but can never be *of* us. We are saved as a consequence of his work and of his gift alone, or we cannot be saved at all.

There are three stages in the assumption by Christ of the office of High Priest -

- ***first:*** he had to be Appointed from among Men, born among us and called out from us as the <u>Incarnate</u> Christ
- ***second:*** he had to Offer an Eternal Sacrifice, which he did at Calvary, when he became the <u>Crucified</u> Christ
- ***third:*** he had to commence Continual Intercession for his people, which began after his resurrection, and is the mark of the <u>Ascended</u> Christ.

All three of those stages are discussed in various parts of this book. They are also reflected in the three books that comprise my trilogy on Christ

Emmanuel	-	the incarnate Christ
The Cross and the Crown	-	the crucified Christ
Highly Exalted	-	the ascended Christ.

"All this has been written down," as David said, "because the hand of the Lord was upon me. My part has been to work out the details of the plan, and to implement it" (1 Ch 28:19). Which is to say, whatever truth is found in these pages must be attributed to God; but any errors are a product of my own inadequacies.

You would probably find it beneficial to read right through the *Letter to the Hebrews* before you go any further into this book.

As you open these pages 1 urge you at least to read the first three and the last two chapters. 1 am sure then you will not be able to resist the urge to plunge into the remainder'.

May the Lord give you joy as you explore the wonders of the ascended Christ and the marvels of his intercessory ministry.

CHAPTER ONE:

ASCENDED

"We, Peter and Paul, do make the following constitutions. Let the slaves work five days; but on the Sabbath-day and the Lord's day let them have leisure to go to church for instruction in piety.

"We have said that the Sabbath is on account of creation, and the Lord's Day of the resurrection. Let slaves rest from their work all the great week, and that which follows it - for the one in memory of the passion, and the other of the resurrection; and if there is need, they should be instructed who it is that suffered and rose again, and who it is permitted him to suffer and raised him again.

"Let them have rest from their work on the Ascension, because it was the conclusion of the dispensation by Christ. Let them rest at Pentecost, because of the coming of the Holy Spirit, which was given to those that believed in Christ."[2]

"Let them have rest from their work on the Ascension ..." Thus wrote the ancient author in his instruction to Christian householders on the way they should treat their slaves. He shows that the early church ranked the day commemorating Christ's Ascension with Christmas, Easter, and others of the greatest days in the Christian calendar. Ascension Day was noteworthy because it marked "the conclusion of the dispensation by Christ" - it was the true culmination of the old era; it opened the way for the new era to begin on the Day of Pentecost.

What do we mean by the "ascension" of Christ? Scripture mentions the event itself in only three places: one that has doubtful authenticity (Mk

---

[2] Constitution of the Holy apostles" 8:4 (33). Translated in "The Anti-Nicene Fathers". Vol 7; Eerdmans Pub. Co. the "Constitutions" are a fourth-century compilation, piously, but falsely attributed to the apostles.

16:19); and two in the writings of Luke. (See Lu 24:51; and Ac [3]1:9, "When he had said this, while they were still watching him, he was lifted up, and a cloud carried him out of their sight." See also vs 22).

Those are the only places where scripture actually tells us what happened.

However, the fact of Christ's ascension was clearly predicted, both in the OT and in the gospels. Everywhere also in Acts and the NT letters the apostles assume that Christ is exalted at the Father's right hand. Even if there were no actual story of the ascension in the NT, we would still infer it from apostolic doctrine.[4]

The ascension took place some 40 days after Jesus' resurrection (Ac 1:3), and the site was Mt Olivet (vs. 12). The disciples watched him rise, enthralled by the spectacle. They ever after rejoiced in the glory of their Lord, and in the benefits that accrued to them from his enthronement. They could never again think of him merely as he was during the years of his incarnation. They could never again doubt that he had truly conquered death, and was now Lord of heaven and earth.

The ascension also closed the post-resurrection appearances of Christ.[5] While the disciples were watching him go up into heaven, two angels spoke to them. "You will not see him again," they said, "until the time comes for his return from heaven. Then he will come again in just the same way as you have seen him go" (see 1:10-11). So they stopped expecting him to keep on appearing to them. From ascension day on, they looked only for his return in glory (Tit 2:13; 2 Pe 3:11-13; Ph 3:20; etc.). His next appearance will be his second coming.[6]

However, the ascension has not isolated Christ from human perception. While it did terminate that once-only revelation of Christ on earth, it also

---

[3] Because of the deficient manuscript support scholars are inclined to feel that neither of those passages were part of the original gospels of Mark and Luke.

[4] The Ascension is <u>anticipated</u> in Jn 6:62; 20:17; and it is affirmed in Ac 2:32-33; Ro 8:34; Cl 3:31; He 1:"3; 6:20; 8:1; 9:12,24; 10:12; 12:2; 13:20; plus many other references, which either declare or imply that Christ is now seated a the Father's right hand in heaven.

[5] Except the special appearance to Paul, Ac 9:3-5

[6] Visions such as John saw on the isle of Patmos, or such as a modern Christian might see, are a different kind of appearance of Christ

opened the way for a universal revelation of Christ - which comes to us through the presence of the Holy Spirit. Indeed, the giving of the Spirit was a direct result of the ascension (Ac 2:32-33). During the years of his incarnation, Jesus could be known by only a few; but now knowledge of him is accessible to every person who receives the witness of the Spirit.

Why was he taken out of their sight "by a cloud"? Here are three suggestions -

(1) Perhaps this was a symbolic way of veiling his divine nature: it hid the change that occurred in him as he rose from an earthly mode of existence into a heavenly one.

(2) The cloud might also have had a more profound significance. I remember reading something that Chrysostom once said. When the disciples witnessed the resurrection, they were permitted to see its end, but not its beginning; but when they witnessed the ascension, they were permitted to see its beginning, but not its end. What might that mean? Chrysostom suggested this: it shows that while the resurrection has been completed, the ascension will not be finalised until the second advent.

(3) C. S. Lewis reflected the opinion of many expositors when he suggested that the "cloud" was not an ordinary cloud, high in the sky. Rather, it was a luminous cloud of glory that gathered quickly around Christ as he lifted away from the disciples.

It may have been similar to the "shekinah" - that mysterious shining cloud that hovered over Israel's tabernacle, and sat between the wings of the cherubim. It covered the ark of the covenant with splendour, and it marked the presence of Yahweh with his people. You might also see an image of the shekinah, and of the cloud that carried him up to heaven, in the "bright cloud" that gathered around Jesus on the mount of transfiguration (Mt 17:5; Mk 9:7; Lu 9:34).

Now notice -

A. THE ASCENSION WAS A SYMBOLIC ACT

Do not suppose that the picture of Christ "ascending" into heaven pre-supposes a childish, outmoded view of the universe - as though the disciples reckoned that heaven was physically above them. Scripture uses the idea of a change of place to suggest a change of state. Many other statements show clearly enough that the biblical writers were aware that heaven is not a particular locality in the sky, but a different dimension altogether.

Nonetheless, as F. F. Bruce comments,

> "Anyone appearing to leave the earth's surface must appear to spectators to be ascending, and so, when the cloud enveloped the visible form of their Lord, his disciples stood `looking steadfastly into heaven as he went'."

It was a natural reaction. Yet on reflection they knew that he had not just kept on travelling upwards. They understood that he had moved out of time into eternity, out of the natural into the spiritual; away from earth and into the wholly different realm of heaven. Therefore, although Christ had departed from them, they knew that he was just as certainly still with them. Indeed, he was more surely with them than he could have been if he had remained confined to the earth (Jn 16:7).

B. IT WAS THE LAST STAGE IN A PROCESS

This ascent of Christ from Olivet was not the first time he had returned to the Father. During the preceding 40 days (between his various resurrection appearances to his disciples) Jesus had been with the Father at heaven's zenith. He did not spend those six weeks locked into some kind of intermediate state - neither in heaven nor on earth. His own words show that on the day of his resurrection he had been with the Father. Do you remember how just after he had risen from the dead he would not allow Mary to touch him? He said, "I have not yet ascended to the Father." Yet "on the evening of the same day" he made himself freely available to his disciples. Apparently, during the hours following his resurrection at dawn and before his evening encounter with the disciples, he had already entered the Father's presence (Jn 20:17-20).

Similarly, Jesus appeared several times to his disciples during the 40 days that stand between his resurrection and his ascension. On those occasions, too, he must have been moving freely between heaven and earth. So then, the event we call the ascension simply fixed the end of those earthly appearances. It firmly established in the minds of the disciples that God had now exalted Christ to his right hand. It was the climax of a process. All others are laid in their native soil; he was carried into the heavens!

C. THE NEED FOR THE ASCENSION

1. His Departure Had to be Known

The appearances of the risen Christ during the 40 days plainly could not continue indefinitely, nor could they stop without explanation, or without some significant terminal happening. If Jesus had just vanished, if the post-resurrection appearances had hazily petered out, confusion and uncertainty would have troubled the disciples.

Barnes writes on the importance of this visible ascent into heaven -

> "It was so arranged as that he should ascend in open day; in the presence of his apostles; and that not when they were asleep or indifferent, but when they were engaged in a conversation that should fix their attention, and when they were looking upon him. Had Jesus vanished secretly, or in the night, the apostles would have been amazed and confounded; perhaps they would even have doubted whether they had not been deceived. But when they saw him leave them in this manner, they could not doubt that he had risen; and when they saw him ascend to heaven, they could not doubt that his work was approved, and that God would carry it onward."[7]

2. Its Power had to be Discovered

We may assert, then, that the visible ascension of Christ established in the minds of the disciples

- the truth of the gospel of salvation; for had he been proclaiming a lie, God would not have honoured him so highly

---

[7] Op. cit., pg. 371. There is a strong echo in this passage of a sermon preached by Chrysostom. The more widely I read the more ruefully I discover that "there is nothing new under the sun". (Ec 1:9). I is a little melancholy to think that I, more than a hundred years after Barnes, have been plodding through the same hours of research (with his pages now added to the list) that Barnes plodded through, just to end up with a paragraph or two! Barnes had only to read Chrysostom to compose his paragraph. I had to read both Chrysostom and Barnes! But cheer up! Perhaps after all there are some things in this book that Barnes never thought of, and perhaps that no-one else has though of – at least, not in the same way.

- the heavenly position of Christ, far above all other dominion, power, and authority; greater than any earthly ruler; greater even than the highest angels
- the satisfactory completion of the work of Christ, for they saw him take into heaven the wounds that were evidence of a finished atonement (Jn 20:20; Re 5:6)
- the nature of his kingdom as a heavenly not earthly, eternal not temporal reign; a monarchy of grace, not force, and of spirit, not flesh
- his identity as universal Lord, not restricted by time, place, nor race (2 Co 5:16)
- the certainty of his majestic return (Ac 1:11).

Christ completed his work of redemption only when he entered heaven bearing in his body the evidence of his atonement. Today his wounds are still visible to the Father's eye, and they will remain so for ever. There is nothing more for Christ to do; nor anything for us to do. The ascension settled the matter. The proof of our salvation is deposited in the heavenlies in Christ, and has become the eternal guarantee of our welcome into the family of God.

CHAPTER TWO:

PROPHESIED

Did heaven reel with astonishment when Jesus returned to his Father's right hand? No, for the event had been long foretold -

FORETOLD BY THE PSALMIST

A. DESTINED TO REIGN

Two famous prophecies of the ascension of Christ stand in the Psalms -

1.   Psalm 24:7-8

Matthew Henry comments -

> "We may apply (those verses) to the ascension of Christ into heaven and the welcome given to him there. When he had finished his work on earth he ascended `in the clouds of heaven'* (Da 7:13-14). The gates of heaven must then be opened to him, those doors that may be truly called `everlasting'*, which had been shut against us, to keep the way of the tree of life (Ge 3:24). Our Redeemer found them shut, but, having by his blood made atonement for sin and gained a title to `enter the holy place'* (He 9:12), as one having authority, he demanded entrance, not for himself only, but for us; for, as the forerunner, he has for us entered and `opened the kingdom of heaven to all believers'*. The keys not only of hell and death, but also of heaven and life, must be put into his hand."[8]

C.H. Spurgeon reckoned that the 24th Psalm was peculiarly "The Song of the Ascension". He says of our text -

> "We have here a picture of our Lord's glorious ascent. We see him rising from *amidst* the little group upon Olivet, and as the cloud receives him, angels reverently

---

[8] Op. cit; in loc.

escort him to the gates of heaven. The ancient gates of the eternal temple are ... called upon to `lift their heads'`, as though with all their glory they were not great enough for the All-glorious King. Let all things do their utmost to honour so great a Prince ... The watchers at the gate hearing the song look over the battlements and ask, `Who is this King of glory?'` A question full of meaning and worthy of the meditations of eternity. Who is he in person, nature, character, office and work? What is his pedigree? What his rank and what his race? The answer given in a mighty wave of music is, `The Lord strong and mighty, the Lord mighty in battle.'` We know the might of Jesus by the battle which he has fought, the victories which he has won over sin, death, and hell, and we clap our hands as we see him leading captivity captive in the majesty of his strength. Oh for a heart to sing his praises! Mighty hero, be thou crowned for ever King of kings and Lord of lords."[9]

The latter part of that quotation echoes a second OT oracle-

2. *Psalm 68:17-18*

In its original setting this psalm probably celebrated the entrance of the Ark of the Covenant into Jerusalem. Paul, however, cites it as an oracle of the ascension of Christ (Ep 4:7-10). To learn what caused him to make that transition and why he quotes the psalm in an altered form, you will need to consult various commentaries. Meanwhile, I will follow Paul, and say that the psalmist's oracle makes three wonderful statements -

B. THE COSMIC DRAMA

The work of Christ can be summarised in three words: he came; he went; he gave. Thus Paul says that

- Christ descended: he came from heaven to earth
- Christ ascended: he rose from earth to heaven
- Christ has given gifts to everyone who believes

---

[9] The Treasury of David", in loc.; 1974 reprint by Zondervan publishing House, Grand Rapids, Michigan; (3 vols.)

1. Christ has DESCENDED

Why did he come? What splendid purpose drove him to forsake the ivory palaces, the supernatural beauty of heaven, and to find a squalid dwelling among mortals? He "descended" indeed - down into the shadows; down into sin; down into disease; down into all the murk of human sorrow! He whose radiance exceeded the glory of a million suns, whose majesty commanded myriads of shining angels, came down, down, down, until he was indistinguishable from a Jewish peasant.

The King of Heaven lived among us as a Galilean carpenter. He whom the mighty and fiery seraphim had once worshipped with joy now dribbled with the spittle of his foes, and stank from the offal they threw into his face.

Yet still he went down, as they tore his flesh with the lash. And down yet more as he, the Prince of Life, humbly yielded himself to death, even the death of the cross.

Again the question: why did he come?

The answer lies in one powerful word: identification. He came to identify himself with those who were to become his friends, though they had once been his enemies. Before Christ came, there was an infinite gulf between God (who is immeasurably good and holy) and man (who is fallen and corrupt). Yet the Father loved us, and deeply yearned to lift us out of sin's darkness and into his sparkling light. He wanted to free us from the dread grip of sickness, to soothe our pain, take away our tears, and turn our weakness into strength. He wanted to fill us with peace, and joy, and prosperity, and to change our defeat into triumph. He wanted us to become identified with him in his divine health, endless wealth, and infinite happiness.

But how could such marvellous changes ever happen to us who were his enemies?

There was only one way: before we could identify ourselves with heaven and its treasures, heaven had to identify itself with us and our poverty.

So Christ came. He came to make himself one with us and our need. He came to overthrow the enemy of our souls, and thus to open a way for us to possess every good gift of God.

Christ became identified with

- your sin, because he was "made sin" (2 Co 5:21).
- your weakness, because he was "crucified in weakness" (13:4).
- your sickness, because it was "the will of the Lord to make him sick" (Is 53:10, RSV margin).
- your poverty, because "for your sake he became poor" (2 Co 8:9).
- your death, because he "poured out his soul to death" (Is 53:12).

All this, so that you and I might become righteous, strong, well, rich in him, and eternally alive!

So he descended, from highest heaven to deepest hades, from loveliest life to ugliest death. But the drama did not end there. Death could not possibly contain him; so the saga continued -

2. *Christ has ASCENDED*

At first sight the statement, "he ascended on high" (Ps 68:18; Ep 4:10), may appear to remove Christ from the human scene, and thus invalidate the results of his previous descent to the earth. But someone cries: "How does the ascension of Christ help me? Has he not gone from the earth, and now dwells gloriously as God in heaven, so far away?" Paul answers by making three statements about the ascended Christ-

a. *"He led captivity captive"*

That striking phrase may mean either

- Jesus is bringing with him into heaven a great host of people who were once captives to sin but are now captives of his love; or,
- Jesus has captured Satan and his hosts, routed the power of sin and death, and cast the devil in fetters before the throne of God.

Some reckon it means the first; others, the second. Either view is valid -

"Prisoners of Love"

It is true that we who believe are now the slaves of Christ - more fully his slaves than we were once slaves of Satan. So we rejoice that he did not return alone to heaven. Instead he brought (and is bringing) with him a vast multitude of willing captives, all singing that "his yoke is easy, and his burden is light!" Or, in the words of the ancient collect: "Thy service is perfect freedom!"

We who are his servants are happy to be chained to his ascending chariot, to be part of his triumphant procession. Does he not carry us from bitter serfdom to the blessed liberty of the sons of God? Onward great Conqueror! Bring us, thy laughing captives, with glad songs to Zion, the city of the Great King (Is 51:11;33:20-22). Our chiefest delight is to serve thee through the eternal ages.

Prisoners of Justice

It is also true that Christ seized the powers of darkness and dragged them in disgrace before the assembled angels of God. He ruined the enemy by turning upon him his own weapons:

- by dying Jesus destroyed death; through burial he entombed the grave;
- by breaking the chains of hades he led captivity captive.

This second view seems the more likely meaning of Paul's quotation, "When he ascended on high he brought a host of captives, and he gave gifts to his people." The captives he harried in bondage; but to his church he gave gifts.

Our ancient foe is now firmly in the grip of Christ; by a just decree he lies imprisoned within the Saviour's will. The Conqueror has nullified his power over the servants of God. We who were once his prisoners now walk freely, loosed by Christ from Satan's charnel. There is now no grave so deep that it lacks a clear path to heaven. The way to paradise lies open to every believer by the resurrection and ascension of Christ -

> "My spirit shall return to Him
> That gave its heavenly spark;
> Yet think not, Sun, it shall be dim
> When thou thyself art dark!
> No! It shall live again and shine
> In bliss unknown to beams of thine,
> By Him recalled to breath
> Who captive led captivity,
> Who robbed the grave of Victory,
> And took the sting from Death!"
>
> - Thomas Campbell, "The Last Man"

b. *"He who ascended also descended"*

Are you anxious lest the ascended Christ is now sitting too high to take notice of mere mortals? Is it possible that his resumption of heavenly splendour has changed him? Banish such thoughts, says Paul. The Jesus who rose is the same as he who loved his disciples, who called them his friends, and swore that he would never forsake them. As he was, so he is and will ever be, Jesus, "the same yesterday, today, and forever" (He 13:8).

If you want to know what he is, simply read the gospels and discover what he was. What he was, he is. Was he Healer then? So is he now. Was he Comforter then? So is he now. Was he Saviour then? So is he now. All that he has ever been, he is still. Whatever he has done, he still does. We may eagerly echo the psalmist -

> *"Our fathers trusted in you; they believed your word, and you rescued them. They cried out to you, and were saved. In you they trusted, and they were not disappointed" (22:4-5).*

So the ascension was an essential precursor to this unchanging ministry of Christ. Before he could be to all disciples what he was to the few who knew him in old Palestine, it was necessary for him to become universally available. Therefore Paul says, thirdly, that because of his ascension -

c. *"Christ fills all things"*

The ascension has not made Christ distant from earth; he has not deserted this planet. On the contrary, he is nearer to us now than he was to those men and women among whom he once lived in the flesh. Now Christ fills the whole earth! How can this be? How does his very closeness to us depend upon the highest exaltation? Because only God is capable of being everywhere at one time. But the elevation of Christ to heaven's loftiest throne has marked him as God. Therefore he must possess the divine attribute of omnipresence, and can say, "Wherever you are, there I will be also!" He holds too the divine attributes of omnipotence and omniscience. Therefore he is a proper focus of worship, one who is able to hear prayer, and to answer it with irresistible might.

Here then is the heavenly paradox: the higher Christ ascends, the nearer he is to us! "But," you might say, "as the Eternal Logos, Christ has always been omnipresent. He never stopped being so, not even during the years of his incarnation."[10]

What then has changed? Why was the ascension necessary?

Answer: Before the resurrection and ascension the Father lacked a legal basis upon which he could justly overthrow Satan and hear the prayers of sinners. Christ was omnipresent as Lord, but not yet as Saviour.

The ascension has changed that. He is still omnipresent as he was before, as the eternal Logos. But now he is with us also in his new identity - the Redeemer and Friend of all who call upon his name. He is not distant, but rather by the side of each believer, in love both willing and able to save.

Three hundred years ago, Sir Roger L'Estrange wrote a poem about an imprisoned royalist who allowed no gaol to deprive him of his liberty to love his king. The poem expresses sentiments that any Christian might echo with greater reality -

> "What though I cannot see my King,
> Either in his person, or in his coin;
> Yet contemplation is a thing
> Which renders what I have not, mine.
> My King from me no adamant can part,
> Whom I do wear engraven in my heart!"

d.   Christ gives GIFTS to his People

What are these gifts? There are many; but here at least are some-

- the gift of his name, by which we have access to the limitless authority of the Christ who bears that name;
- the gift of his church, against which the gates of hell cannot prevail, and in which each Christian has an appointed office (1 Co 12:27-28; Ro 12:4-5);
- the gift of his Spirit, by which we receive power to be his witness, and through which we have access to various other supernatural gifts (1 Co 12:7-11; Ro 12:6-8);
- the gift of his ministers, whom Paul singles out as the preeminent boon of the ascended Christ, for through them Christ himself continues to minister in the church (Ep 4:11).

[10] See my discussion of this idea in the book "Emmanuel".

Bengel claims that there is fine poetry and proportion in Paul's Greek original of this passage (Ep 4:11-16). Bengel's commentary is lengthy, but I think he would summarise the passage as follows, setting it out in three triple paragraphs -

> The Office of Ministry (vs 12)
>
> > Christ gave ministry-gifts to the church
> >
> > > for the perfecting of the saints
> > unto the work of the ministry
> > > unto building up the body of Christ
>
> The Goal of the Saints (vs 13)
> Until we have all arrived
> > at the unity of the faith
> to mature manhood
> > to the fulness of Christ
>
> The Way of Growth (vs 14-16)
>
> In order that we may no longer be infants
> blown about by every wind of doctrine; (vs 14) but
> > speaking the truth in love we may grow (vs 15)
> > being fitted and brought together (vs 16)

A church moving in the life of the ascended Christ will allow him to place in it each of his ministry gifts (apostles, prophets, evangelists, pastors, and teachers). Only by the presence of these ministries can "the saints be equipped for the work of ministry" that Christ has given each of them. Furthermore, this coming together of ascension-gift ministries with the ministering saints brings a new force into the world. It is the secret that enables the church truly to be "the body of Christ" in the world (vs 12-13). That is, these ministries shape the church to be to each local community what Jesus himself would be, if he were here in the flesh.

Concerning the gift of ministers, that fiery Puritan John Owen once wrote -

> "It will one day appear that there is more glory, more excellency, in giving one poor minister unto a congregation, by furnishing him with spiritual gifts for the discharge of his duty than in the pompous instalment of a thousand popes, cardinals, or metropolitans. The

worst of men, in the observance of a few outward rites and ceremonies, can do the latter; Christ only can do the former, and that because he is ascended up on high to that purpose."[11]

We need not accept Owen's disbelief that Christ could be present at the installation of a pope to allow the truth of his larger claim: only Christ can call and equip a true minister of the gospel. The prerogative of giving apostles, prophets, evangelists, pastors, teachers, to the church belongs wholly to the Master. No one can arrogate to himself a divine mission, nor the charismatic equipment to fulfil that mission. Many have attempted to do so, but the result is always spiritual death for the church. What is born of the flesh stays flesh, and it will perish; only what is born of the Spirit can minister endless life. Hence the Lord spoke with anger -

> *"I did not send these prophets yet they ran; I did not speak to them, yet they prophesied" (Je 23:21).*

Let every person who claims to be a minister of Christ ensure that he truly is one whom Christ himself has sent. Let the church accept none as its minister unless it sees in that person the signs of divine endowment and divine mission. Lacking all other endowments, but possessing the charisma of Christ, the minister may serve the church fruitfully. If he (or she) possesses all other endowments except the charisma of Christ, the minister cannot do other than construct a body of lifeless clay.

FORETOLD BY JESUS

All the major predictions Jesus made about his ascension are recorded by John - 3:13; 6:62; 7:33; 14:28-29; 16:5; 20:17. This is one of several indicators of the difference in focus that exists among the gospels. Matthew, Mark, and Luke concentrate upon the incarnate Christ; but John has his eye fixed more upon the pre-existent and now glorified Christ.

The next chapter takes up this theme of the exalted Christ.

---

[11] Quoted in the "Treasury of David", on Ps 68:17.

CHAPTER THREE:

EXALTED

Here is excitement! Here is an explosion of spiritual power! When Jesus told his disciples about his approaching return to his Father's right hand, he was not reciting a pretty doctrine. Rather, he set before them a cornucopia of promises that would for ever transform them![12] He wanted them to understand what they should learn from his ascension. So he linked with that great event the following ideas:

- the authority of his teaching;
- the new birth;
- revelation of his real identity;
- confirmation of his prophetic words;
- the giving of the Holy Spirit;
- unshakeable joy;
- his high priestly ministry.
- but mostly, a vision of

HIS HEAVENLY EXALTATION

A. A GREAT GLORY

Jesus himself interpreted his ascension as an "entrance into glory"; that is, an exaltation to the place of supreme power and dignity (Lu 24:26). Paul expressed the same idea -

> *"By the exercise of his limitless strength, God raised Jesus from the dead and enthroned him in the heavenlies at his own right hand, far above all other authority, government, power and dominion, and above every title that has ever been claimed, not only in this world, but also in that which is to come."[13]*

---

[12] See again the list at the end of the previous chapter, and also the references discussed below

[13] Ep 1:20-21a; and see also 4:10; 3:1; 1 Ti 3:16; He 4:14; Ac 7:55

To that picture we could add the splendid scenes of the Apocalypse. John gives a stunning vision of the glorified Christ and of his actions from the throne; but see especially Re 3:21; 5:6-14; 7:17; 14:14. Each of those passages shows Christ sitting with indescribable majesty at the right hand of the Father.

Then there is Paul's arresting phrase, "God has super-exalted Christ and bestowed on him the name that is above every name" Ph 2:9). He employs an intensified compound verb, which expresses exaltation in the highest degree. It is impossible to imagine anything higher. Paul wants to show that Christ's present state is (in a mysterious way) even more exalted than the state he had with the Father before his incarnation (vs 6-7).

He was exalted before; but now he is super-exalted. What has given the Man of Galilee this astonishing pre-eminence? Two things:

- **first,** there is the human nature the Logos assumed in the incarnation, which (to the wonderment of the heavenly hosts) he has now taken into heaven; and
- **second,** there is the new identity he now has: as Redeemer; as Head of the church, which is his body; as Chief Shepherd; as High Priest for ever after the order of Melchizedek; and so on (He 7:1 ff.; 1 Pe 5:4; etc).

So there is a quality about Christ since his ascension that has added a new lustre to his being. He now bears a splendour that compels both the angels and the redeemed saints to sing his praise. With glad voices they raise a paean that exceeds all the anthems of the prior ages (cp. Re 5:8-14).

Now this raises an intriguing question: how does the human nature of Jesus fit into this exaltation?

There must be a sense in which the body of Jesus, taken up into heaven, remains localised. I mean, it remains confined to a single place, it exists within boundaries, it still has shape and definition. We cannot suppose that a once-physical body could ever take on the infinite quality of divine omnipresence. Yet there must be some part of Jesus' human nature that has now been taken fully into the Logos. When he said, "I am with you always," he did not mean just himself as the Logos, but as the Logos in union with Jesus of Nazareth. He would be with them as the Master whom they had known and loved, whom they could readily recognise (Lu 24:36-39).

There is a mystery here, which it may not be profitable to pursue. As Augustine once wrote -

B. A GREAT MYSTERY

> "The question as to where and what manner the Lord's body is in heaven, is one which it would be altogether over-curious and superfluous to prosecute. Only we must believe that it is in heaven. For it pertains not to our frailty to investigate the secret things of heaven, but it does pertain to our faith to hold elevated and honourable sentiments on the subject of the Lord's body."[14]

The church has never been able to show without doubt how to resolve this mystery. But at least we must hold to two ideas -

(1) that the body of Jesus is in heaven, in a spiritual form, yet somehow with spatial boundaries; and

(2) that Christ must absolutely possess the attributes of deity, while retaining his new identity as the God-man.

We cannot wholly separate his humanity from his deity, as though only the Logos is with us; on the contrary, it is Jesus who is with us. Yet neither can we attribute deity to his human nature alone, as though it were only Jesus who is with us, for he can be everywhere present only as the eternal Logos.

There is a vivid reflection of this mystery in the remarkable way Jesus once described his relationship with the Holy Spirit. It seems that the Spirit integrates himself with the revelation of Jesus to the believer, and with the believer's sense of the presence of Christ.

Look at the following list from the gospel of John -

- 14:16 "The Father will give you another Comforter"
- 14:18 "I will not leave you in despair; I will come to you"
- 14:25 "The Father will send the Holy Spirit in my name"
- 14:28 "I am going away, and I will come to you"

[14] "On Faith and the Creed", ch. 16, #13

- 15:26 "I will send the Comforter to you from the Father ... The Spirit of truth proceeds from the Father ... He will bear witness of me"
- 16:7 "I will send the Comforter to you"
- 16:13 "When the Spirit of truth comes, he will glorify me"
- 16:16 "In a little while you will see me"

There seems a strange confusion in those statements. Who is sending the Spirit upon the church? Is it the Father? Or Jesus? Or is the Spirit descending of his own accord?

Again, who is actually coming to the church? Is it the Spirit? Or Jesus? For in one breath, Jesus said that he himself would come, but in the next, that the Spirit would come.

Notice that the day of Pentecost saw both promises fulfilled. So Christ came to the church, and upon the church, in the person of the Spirit. But who then came? The Spirit? Or Jesus?

Or again, scripture says that it is the task of the Spirit to reveal Jesus, and to glorify Jesus in the church. Yet there is more than that, for it is not just the Spirit who comes, but Jesus himself.

So an impenetrable mystery confronts us. Any attempt to meld these statements succeeds only at the cost of weakening them into flaccidness.

No doubt Jesus was aware of this. Yet he offered no clarification of his meaning. Why? Perhaps because it lies beyond the power of human language, or even human thought, to describe the infinite mystery of the Godhead. Ultimately the being of God, and the relationship between Father, Son, and Holy Spirit, must remain undiscoverable by mortals.

However, the way Jesus spoke does show firmly that the Holy Spirit works constantly to reveal on earth the ascended Christ in all his deity, and in all his humanity.

THE MANNER OF HIS EXALTATION

A. AN INCOMPARABLE HONOUR

Who can tell the splendour of this Saviour of ours? He is -

1. Exalted in Title

"God has bestowed on him the highest possible title, so that at the name of Jesus every knee should bow, whether in heaven, or on earth, or under the earth. And every tongue must also proclaim that Jesus Christ is Lord, to the glory of God the Father (Ph 2:9-11).

2. Exalted in Office

"God has elevated Jesus to his right hand, making him both Commander and Saviour ... Christ is the Head of the church, his body, and is himself its Saviour" (Ac 5:31; Ep 5:23).

3. Exalted in Authority

"For this purpose Christ died and lived again, so that he might be Lord both of the dead and of the living ... You have come to complete life in him, who is Supreme over all dominion and authority" (Ro 14:9; Cl 2:10).

4. Exalted in Position

Christ now sits enthroned at the right hand of God (see Mk 16:19; Ac 2:33; 7:55,56; Ro 8:34; Cl 3:1; He 10:12; 1 Pe 3:22; plus several other references. The idea behind that expression is one of equality (cp. 1 Kg 2:19). If Christ sits beside the Father, then God honours him as an equal, and fully shares with his Son his limitless dominion.

5. Exalted as Judge

The ascension of Christ has marked him as the one "ordained by God to judge the living and the dead" (Ac 10:42; 2 Co 5:9-10). Who can measure the greatness of Christ? Who could ever tell his majesty and glory? Exalted so high! So magnificent in power! Yet still our Lover and Saviour. We dare to sing with that unknown saint who long ago rejoiced: "O happy fault, which has deserved to have such and so mighty a Redeemer!"

B. SITTING ON THE THRONE

"When Jesus had won purification from all sin, he was enthroned at the right hand of the Majesty on high" (He 1:3).

Could you find a statement more redolent with awe? Can you not sense how his glorious majesty defies human imagination? Yet we must try to gaze upon his dazzling splendour and to understand what it means for us.

Some have argued: if Christ sits at God's right hand, then he must be a localised being and thus distinct from God, who is universal. Surely they have forgotten the obvious? If the statement limits Christ by giving him a specific locality, it must equally do the same to the Father - else it were impossible for the one to sit at the right hand of the other! If sitting on the throne restricts the Son, it does so just as surely for the Father. Hence Augustine wrote in the 4th century

> "If we take it carnally, then because (Christ) sitteth on the right hand of the Father, the Father will be on his left hand. Is it consistent with piety so to put them together, the Son on the right, the Father on the left? There it is all right hand, because no misery is there.

So we must allow a symbolic sense for the expression, "Christ is sitting at God's right hand." Yet the image still has strong meaning. It shows that there is a special locality, a central place of divine government, situated somewhere beyond the universe, called "on high". There God has established his throne; there the angels have concourse; and from there the Father and the Son exercise their distinctive administrations.

To that place the angels saw Christ ascend and take his seat in matchless splendour. To that place the eye of faith turns, for it is made visible by scripture and by revelation of the Spirit. There we see Christ, ascended, sitting, glorious, yet still bearing the likeness of a man; in fact, of a crucified man. In this vision we discover -

C. THE MESSAGE OF THE THRONE

How many are the powerful spiritual blessings that come to us from the ascension of Christ! Here are some of them -

1. God Identified with His People

Here is the central lesson of the ascension. Christ assumed human form so that in life and death he might suffer extreme humiliation. But now he has taken that same nature to the pinnacle of heaven, where it enjoys the staggering honour of being next to God! Credulity reels! Astonishment grips even the holy angels -

"What is man that you should take any notice of him? ...
For a little while you ranked him lower than the angels;
but now you have crowned him with glory and honour,
putting everything in total subjection to him" (He 2:6-8,
and context).

The disciples watched Jesus, their familiar companion and teacher, ascend into heaven. They caught the stunning truth that humanity is now irrevocably identified with deity. The incarnation depicted the humiliation of God; the ascension depicts the glorification of humanity. Christ enthroned in heaven guarantees that all whom the blood of the lamb washes clean will stand closer to the throne of God than do the lovely cherubim. Even the mighty seraphim must still cover their faces (Is 6:2). But we with "open faces" will continue to "look upon the glory of the Lord, changing continually into his likeness from glory to glory" (2 Co 3:18).

So the ascension has confirmed the wondrous identification of our humanity with deity. Now and forever, an indissoluble union exists between God and redeemed humankind! If the incarnation spoke of the humiliation of God, then the ascension speaks of the glorification of the believer!

Thus Augustine wrote -

"In order to give man's mind greater confidence in its journey toward the truth along the way of faith, God the Son of God, who is himself the Truth, took manhood without abandoning his Godhead, and thus established and founded this faith, so that man might have a path to man's God through the man who was God. For this is `the mediator between God and man, the man Christ Jesus' (1 Ti 2:5). As man he is our Mediator; for as man he is our way. For there is hope to attain a journey's end when there is a path which stretches between the traveller and his goal. But if there is no path, or if a man does not know which way to go, there is little use in knowledge of the destination. As it is, there is one road, and one only, well secured against all possibility of going astray, and the road is provided by the one who is both himself God and man. As God, he is the goal; as man, he is the way."[15]

2. The Way to Honour is Abasement

The ascension shows that the true way to honour is the way of abasement (Ph 2:5,9). A true vision of the ascension will destroy the urge to accumulate earthly treasures. Where Christ is, in heaven, now becomes our only valid goal, hope, joy, and wealth (Cl 3:1-3).

3. Two key words

The ascension identifies this age as the age of faith and patience. Two words characterise the new era

a. Separation

"While he was still blessing them he was separated from them and carried up into heaven" (Lu 24:51).

"Separation" is the first word associated in scripture with the ascension. It identifies this age as one of loneliness, and of the struggle of faith. Christ is parted from us. We cannot see him, nor handle him. The call now comes to us: stand by faith, not depending upon either sight or feeling (2 Co 5:7).

Of course, Christ is actually nearer to us than our own bodies; but that is a faith perception. To our natural senses he seldom seems so close, and often we feel desperately alone: "The eternal silence of these infinite spaces terrifies me."[16] Sometimes those "spaces" exist in the endless universe beyond me; sometimes they lie in the measureless depths of my own soul. Sometimes it is the outer world that refuses me any reply; sometimes my own spirit feels surrounded by everlasting silence. But when both the inner and outer universes stand empty and silent to the spirit, then truly our most needed quality is faith. When God and Christ seem to have abandoned you, that is when you most need to stand on the scripture. The clouds may have parted Jesus from human sight (Ac 1:9), but we are not alone. Has he not promised never to forsake us? (Mt 28:20; He 13:5-6)

---

[15] City of God; ed. By David Kowles; Penguin Classics, 1972; Bk 11, ch 2.

[16] Pascal, op. cit., #392

b. *Waiting*

> *"You are serving the living and true God, while you are*
> *waiting for his Son to come from heaven, whom he*
> *raised from the dead - Jesus, who is our Saviour from*
> *the coming day of wrath" (1 Th 1:9-10).*

This age of separation will not last for ever; for while Christ is presently parted from us, we are also waiting for him to appear again. "This Jesus," said the angels, "who was taken up from you into heaven, will come in the same way as you saw him go into heaven" (Ac 1:11). The ascension, then, was not an end, but the beginning of the signs of the second advent. There are those who believe that now, after nearly twenty centuries, the days of waiting must be nearly ended, that Christ must soon return. May the event prove them right! But there are also those who believe that twenty more centuries may have to pass by before Christ will come in his glory.

Yet whether his return is near or far, the call remains unchanged: wait with patient faith (see also 1 Co 1:7-9).

Yet he asks us to do no more than he is doing himself, for he too is waiting (He 10:12-13). Waiting to subdue his enemies. Waiting for the Father to speak the word that will release him to return for his waiting church (Mt 24:36). Waiting to celebrate a joyous marriage to his beautiful Bride (Re 19:7). Waiting for the glad supper that will follow (vs 9), when he himself, with unimaginable love and grace, will serve at the table (Lu 12:37). Waiting to inaugurate his millennial kingdom, full of peace, from which will be banished all iniquity and pain.

Yes, he is waiting. Calmly. Patiently. Waiting for the Father's will, which is his will. The time of his ascension is a waiting time. Heaven and earth together, God and the church, all "waiting expectantly for our marvellous hope, when the glory of our great God and Saviour Jesus Christ will be seen by all" (Tit 2:13).

Yet while we wait with Christ for the Father to speak the word that will bring time to an end, we do not sorrow. Loneliness and sorrow are not the only characteristics of this ascension age. It is also the era of

(i) *Blessing*

At their last sight of Jesus, during his final moments with them, the disciples saw him with his hands lifted up and "blessing" them. In this attitude he parted from them, and was carried up into heaven - see Lu 24:50-51. What a marvellous scene! How often they must have reminded each other of those incredible moments, and of the rich promise conveyed by those uplifted hands, and by the words of blessing. The memory of his vanishing figure forced upon them a startling realisation. Far from limiting the blessing they could receive from God, the ascension had made available to them vastly greater treasures of divine grace!

So great was the impact of the ascension upon them that none of the disciples ever yearned to turn time back to the days when Jesus was with them in the flesh. On the contrary, although they had once known Christ "according to the flesh", now they no longer looked at him from such an earthy point of view. Instead, they rejoiced to know that he had passed into the heavens, with hands outstretched forever to bless his people! (2 Co 5:16)

(ii) Joy and Worship

Immediately after the disciples had seen Jesus ascend into heaven, "*they returned to Jerusalem with surpassing joy, and were constantly blessing God in the temple*" (Lu 24:52-53). For those who have discovered life in Christ, the ascension brings its marvellous payload of joy and worship. We worship him because the ascension confirmed beyond any further doubt his divine identity. We rejoice because, knowing that he sits at God's right hand, we als-o know that there is no limit to his ability. He can easily fulfil every promise he ever made. Nor can anyone suppose that he who sits so high would ever stoop to deceit. None will ever see his shadow moving here and there like that of a man who constantly changes direction (Jas 1:17). His face is fixed toward his people; according to his total power, he is always looking to do them good.

c.   The ascension is now

Have you ever pondered this? The ascension is the only part of the passion of Christ in which we are actual participants.

Alone of the acts that comprised the drama of Jesus' life on earth, the ascension is still happening. We must talk about each of his other acts in the past tense: descended, conceived, born, lived, suffered, crucified, died, buried and raised again. But the ascension is in the present tense -

"Christ ... who sits at the right hand of God, and is always pleading our cause!" (Ro 8:34) ... "Set your heart upon those things that are above, where Christ is, seated at God's right hand" (Cl 3:1) ... "Fix your eye on Jesus ... who is seated at the right hand of the throne of God" (He 12:2) ... "Christ has gone into heaven and now sits at the right hand of God, where all angels, rulers, and powers are subservient to him" (1 Pe 3:22).

We might say: "He came. He sits. He will come." We were not here when he came. We may not be here when he comes. But we are here now, during the years of his ascension, living in his presence while he sits at the Father's right hand. The ascension is the one part of the redemption drama during which we ourselves live! It is happening NOW! And see how serenely he sits - untroubled, certain of triumph -

"When Christ had offered for all time a single sacrifice for sins, he sat down at the right hand of God, and now he is waiting for all his enemies to become his footstool" (He 10:12-13).

The same serenity should characterise us during this era of the ascension.

CHAPTER FOUR:

GRACIOUS

Christ was our pioneer. He entered heaven for us as a fore-runner, a scout, an advance agent - see Hebrews 4:14; 6:19-20; 12:2. He showed that it is possible for someone in human form to enter the holiest place in the universe and to stand at the summit of power. He has blazed a trail for us to follow.

That by itself is a marvellous feat. Yet it has another fine aspect. The presence in heaven of the human nature of Jesus enables him to be our high priest. He could not be our priest if he were not one of us (He 2:17). He could not represent us before God if he did not wear our likeness. But he is indeed our fellow, and he stands as priest between us and God, interceding for us -

CHRIST OUR GREAT HIGH PRIEST

"We have a great high priest who has passed through the heavens - Jesus, the Son of God. Therefore we should cling tightly to our profession of faith (He 4:14).

A. JESUS IS OUR PRIEST

People have always needed a priest to stand apart from them and in their stead to stand in the presence of the Deity. That need has allowed Satan to create one of his deadliest snares - a corrupted priesthood. Consequently, those priests who should have been their people's best benefactors been rather their most vicious tormentors.

We have a word in our language: "priest-craft". It means "the material policy of a priesthood", and it usually carries an ill-omened sense: "the scheming of selfish and ambitious priests to gain wealth and power". Sadly, this has too often been the case. Priests have used their calling to abuse the credulity of the very people they were meant to serve. How could this happen?

"Priest" (in Greek) simply means "sacred" or "holy". It implies that the priest is neither profane nor defiled. Therefore he has permission to stand where others, without him, would not dare stand. He may enter where they are forbidden. He may approach the throne in a way that for them would bring death.

Can any man or woman be found who possesses such holiness innately? Unfortunately, they cannot. Therefore among the Jews, priests had to be hallowed by ceremonial means. No other method was possible. The result was perhaps inevitable: priestly consecrations were often superficial. No improvement occurred in the moral character of the priest. He felt no ethical compulsion to fulfil his duties honourably.

But Jesus is all that a priest should be; he fulfils every requirement of both heaven and earth. In place of our profanity he is holy, and he is sacred in place of our defilement. He stands where we would not dare stand. He may enter where ruin would swallow us. He intervenes between us and God; he takes our worship and clothes it with fragrance, so making it acceptable to heaven. As a Priest, he has fulfilled for us all the sacred rites of God's law.

B. JESUS IS OUR HIGH PRIEST

Christ is not only Priest, he is also

- High Priest, and therefore able to offer sacrifice for the whole nation
- High Priest, and therefore free to enter the holiest place;
- High Priest, and therefore holds ascendancy over all other priests;
- High Priest, and therefore competent to offer sacrifice for other priests.

The Bible says that we who believe in Christ have ourselves become "priests" before God. As priests, we may offer certain sacrifices to God - of prayer, praise, petition, both on our own behalf and for others. But sacrifice for sin, atonement for sin, we cannot make, for that is the prerogative of the High Priest alone. Yet we are no poorer for that limit. Christ has so gloriously completed the work of redemption that no one can do anything more.

C. JESUS IS OUR GREAT HIGH PRIEST

In the past, to suit their own decay, people frequently chose their priests from the lowest of men. So it happened in Israel, when Jeroboam "appointed the meanest of the people to be priests of the high places".

Sometimes men have arrogated to themselves the office of high priest: *"anyone who wanted the office was consecrated to it by the king, and he became one of the priests of the high places"* (1 Kg 13:33). The Bible then says, "this wicked behaviour led to the downfall of the House of Jeroboam, caused its complete ruin, and the annihilation of the family line." The office of priest is a sacred one; it cannot be assumed lightly. Godless and careless people who debase the priesthood will surely incur heaven's wrath.

How differently God has behaved. When he wished to appoint a Priest who could act for all people, he chose a true High Priest, in fact, a Great High Priest: Jesus, the Eternal One. He is a Great High Priest because:

(1) He alone has the right to decide who will stand before God and who will be rejected. Jesus said, "No one knows the Father, except the Son and those to whom he chooses to reveal the Father" (Mt 11:27).

(2) He is far above any other. He is powerful. He cannot be measured. He is great because he has proclaimed a great Gospel, and has shown great grace. He had no beginning and will have no end. His dominion is vast, his glory ineffable, his lineage divine. His worship is the chief worship, his salvation is the principal matter, his church is the most noble, his calling the most dignified. He is great because of the excellency of his nature, the immensity of his love, the majesty of his throne, the eminence of his authority. Especially, he is greater than all priests. Why? Every former high priest had to slip from life with his labour unfinished, his ambitions undone, his people still chained by sin. But Christ lives for ever, and his ministry will never be diminished.

(3) "He has passed through the heavens." The heavens were too small for Jesus. Jesus was too big for the heavens. They could not encompass him. He passed through them. He went beyond them. He passed through the starry heavens above us. He passed through the heavens of the angels' dwelling. He passed through the infinite regions beyond. He passed into the realm of the "Majesty on High". No man ever did this; but revelation attests that Jesus did.

(4) He is "Jesus, the Son of God," a phrase that compels our attention again to the brilliant unfolding of the glory of Christ that blazes in every page of the Gospel. Our High Priest is Jesus, a name that is "more excellent" than the names of the bright angels (1:4). Our High Priest is Jesus the Son of God, already shown by the apostle to be the Creator, equal with God, better than the angels, better than Moses, better than Joshua.[17]

(5) He opened up the heavens for us. It says, "since we have ... " At this present moment, you and I have a great High Priest, whom we may "see" whenever we please. Not in the sense of viewing him with our eyes, but that we have constant and easy access to him. "Since Jesus has passed through the heavens, let us keep looking to him!" He broke open the brassy roof that hid the heavens from us. His strong arm tossed every barrier aside. He passed through and made the way open for us. Lewi Pethrus says that now we are "living under an open heaven". Hence Paul could write to the Ephesians -

> *"Blessed be the God and Father of our Lord Jesus Christ who has blessed us with every spiritual blessing in the heavenlies in Christ ... He has also lifted us up with Christ and enthroned us with him in the heavenlies" (1:3;2:6).*

Here is a strange thing: while we are still here on earth, we have yet entered into the heavenlies with Christ!

Lewi Pethrus says,

> "It should be possible to apply to the entire Christian Church the confession of Stephen, *'Behold, I see the heavens opened, and the Son of Man standing on the right hand of God'* (Acts 7:56). The early Christian Church lived literally under an open heaven. In Old Testament days, there were three rooms in the tabernacle. The first was the *outer court*, the second the *holy place* where the priests entered and performed their daily service, and the third was the *holy of holies* where only the high priest entered once a year with the blood of the sin offering. The holy of holies is a type of heaven

---

[17] See the earlier chapter of Hebrews

itself, where Christ, after his death and resurrection, entered to appear in our behalf. The holy place is symbolic of the present time. It is a type of the Christian Church of our day. The true holy of holies is in heaven and the holy place is the Church on earth. These correspond to the two rooms of the tabernacle which were next to each other.

"That which separated these two rooms was the veil; but when Jesus died it was rent in twain from the top to the bottom. This occurrence corresponds with a wonderful reality in the spiritual world. Now there is no veil to separate heaven's holy of holies from the Church on earth. We are exhorted to come boldly before the throne of grace in the holy of holies to find grace to help in time of need.

"Heaven's holy of holies and the Church on earth are now one and the same room. The saints have access to heaven itself, and God dwells in the midst of his people. This must become a living reality to you! That which was most remarkable with respect to Stephen's vision was not that heaven was open, because this it always is above the soul that believes in Jesus - but the wonderful thing was that he saw it open. Many a time we stand beneath an open heaven when we are of the opinion that we stand before an open hell. We think that the evil will swallow us up, but, in reality, heaven is open. If Stephen had looked around, he perhaps would have seen hell open to receive him, but he looked upward and saw heaven open. It is just this that we should do - not look at the things about us, but look upward and reckon with heavenly things.

"There are those who sing, `Rend the heavens and come down.' But we need not pray thus longer, for the heavens have been rent and God has not come down. This took place when Jesus came and, through his death and resurrection, opened a way into heaven itself and, at the same time, opened the way for heaven to come into contact with people on earth."[18]

(6) "Since we have such a great High Priest, let us cling tightly to our profession of faith" (Heb 4:14)

(a) What are we to hold onto tightly? "Our profession of faith" in Christ. That is, if we admit the truth of the Gospel and no longer wish to quarrel with God, let us put some strength into our faith through a bold testimony. The idea is that we must make a covenant with the Lord, assent to his will, and acknowledge him not merely as Saviour but also as Lord. Further, it means to declare publicly your faith in his redeeming work and to assert your trust in his mercy and grace.

Those who truly profess Christ claim boldly to be children of God and citizens of the heavenly kingdom. Their speech is a constant affirmation of a holy nature, and of an expressed desire for goodness. Their words show an undying love affair with righteousness. Those who are "clinging tightly to their profession of faith" are people who have spoken a solemn oath of faith in Christ, and have sworn unfaltering allegiance to him.

(b) We must "cling tightly" to this profession. That is, we must exert all the spiritual, mental and physical strength we possess, and every resource at our disposal to seize hold of it and retain it. Our lives must be moulded to its pattern. We should so grip our testimony of faith and be so firmly rooted in Christ that no trial, nor temptation, nor opposition, could ever cause us to move away from the hope of the gospel. We should fortify our lives and secure our defences against any possible approach of evil or onslaught of Satan, lest we lose our profession and so incur the wrath of this High Priest who is so great.

Do you want to please him? Then diligently search to the depths of gospel truth and dig deep into the foundations of the scripture. Be fixed in your resolve to trust Christ, constant in your determination to serve Christ, stable in your witness for Christ, and unswerving in your devotion to the church of Christ.

Unlike the manna of old, which quickly rotted, the experience of those who cling to Christ constantly renews itself. Adhering closely to the Saviour, their victory and joy are durable, abounding more each day.

---

[18] I have lost the source of this quote

CHRIST - OUR GRACIOUS HIGH PRIEST

- see He 4:15-16

It is wonderful to know the greatness of Jesus, but this very fact seems to make him unapproachable. Here is a trembling soul in need of mercy, grace, and help. A priest such as Aaron could be spoken to and his help solicited. But how can a sinner speak to Jesus, the glorious Son of God? Surely his very eminence makes him of less value to us than Aaron? No, says the apostle, far from it. In Jesus we have a High Priest who has "felt the pain of all our frailties".

Could there be a more encouraging affirmation? Two things stand out: Christ has felt our pain; Christ still feels our pain –

1. Christ has felt our pain

That is, he has suffered under the impact of every temptation to which we are subject:

- he knows the temptation of power, for he said that 12 legions of angels were at his disposal;
- he knows the temptation of poverty, for he said, "The Son of Man has nowhere to lay his head;"
- he knows the temptation of wealth, for all the kingdoms of the world and all the glory of them were offered to him;
- he knows the temptation of weakness, for he cried, "I thirst!"
- he knows the temptation of sin, for "he was made sin for us";
- he knows the temptation of sickness, for "he himself carried our diseases and bore our sicknesses".

Further, because Christ was perfect and his emotions and understanding undarkened by sin, he knew the biting strength of temptation more than any other sufferer. There is no feeling, no weakness, no sorrow, no infirmity to which we are subject that did not strike him with full force.

Yet he remained "without sin"; or, more literally, "apart from sin". This is one thing Christ did not experience within himself - the deep shame of sin, the awful sense of failure, the instinct of impending doom. Yet even here God made his Son to feel the pain of these things. For a moment on the cross, while Jesus grappled with the horror of darkness that was settling upon him, the Father forsook his Son. Wracked by the torment of that dreadful abandonment, the Saviour cried, "My God! Why have you forsaken me?" Why? Why? No one will ever fully understand that dark hour, or the purpose of it, or Jesus' cry of anguish. But this at least is part of the answer. Up to that time, Jesus had experienced every temptation and infirmity of human life, apart from the inner guilt of sin. But here the Father made his Son feel even that - made him suffer even that bleak despair - so that for us he might be a perfect High Priest.

2.   *Christ still feels our pain*

Unlike many priests before him, or after him, Christ is always willing to hear, always willing to sympathise, always filled with compassion, always able to understand. He has a fellow-feeling with his people; his mercy flows out to them freely. All who come to Jesus will find a High Priest who is tender and kind, willing to pity them and to let their hurt touch him. He knows our infirmities and is gracious toward our weakness. He knows our frailty and is gentle toward our faults.

Never be afraid then to come to him, for he is a *"merciful and faithful High Priest, who himself suffered under temptation, and so is able to succour those who are tempted"* (He 2:18).

CHAPTER FIVE:

SUPERIOR

What makes a priest? What does a priest have to be and do? The apostle reckons that three things are essential -

THE CHARACTERISTICS OF AARON

- see Hebrews 5:1-4

A. APPOINTED FOR THE PEOPLE

> *"A high priest is ordained to act as the representative of his people in everything that pertains to God" (v 1).*

Primarily he is appointed to "offer gifts, and sacrifices for sin". Why cannot the people bring their own offerings? Because the tarnish of sin lies upon both them and their gifts. Therefore the ministry and altar of a priest are necessary to sanctify each sacrifice, and so make it acceptable to God. Sinners need a hand other than their own to make reparation for their sin.

To offer the gifts of the people to God, and to present sacrifice for them, has always been the major duty of a priest. Therefore, because God has provided us with a perfect High Priest, we know that he expects gifts and sacrifices from us.

But what can we possibly offer him?

What gift has sufficient value, what sacrifice sufficient force, to blot out the memory of our transgressions? Certainly nothing that our own hands could fashion.

Are we then destitute?

No, for Jesus has constituted himself the one eternal gift and the one eternal sacrifice. Because of that, and under the covering of his perfect work, such gifts and sacrifices as we are able to present are suddenly ennobled. Taken up by his hand, and presented to the Father, our offerings, which otherwise would be worthless, gain infinite value.

B. APPOINTED FROM AMONG THE PEOPLE

A priest must be one with his people in nature and experience; he must be "chosen from among them" (vs. 1). How else could the people trust their representative to show "patient sympathy toward the wayward and ignorant"? How could an exotic priest establish rapport with the people? He has no relationship with them; how could he convey true empathy?

But then another question presses forward: what value is a priest who is a friend to his fellows, yet a stranger to God? Indeed, a genuine priest must perfectly know God and perfectly understand the people. His task is twofold: to draw men and women to God; and in turn to bring God to them.

Were any of the ancient priests able to fulfil that double demand? Yes, if they were true priests, "ordained" by God. Their ordination marked them as men known by God, and it called them to the knowledge of God. Of each high priest who responded heartily to the divine investment the people could say:

- he is permanently set in the presence of God;
- he is the appointed bearer of the sacred office;
- he is designated our representative before God;
- he is constituted the representative of God before us;
- he is the medium by whom God conveys his message to us;
- he is set apart as a minister of holy things;
- he is established as the servant of God;
- but most important of all, he is able to know us because "he too is enclosed within frailty".

Because, like his people, he was human, weakness and sickness surrounded the priest. Wherever he looked, in his own home and beyond, he saw the evidence of sin and the need of sacrifice. He was himself bound by infirmity, hampered by evil, restricted by feebleness.

This fact, that infirmity besets every high priest taken from his fellows, leads to two results:

first: he is able to have compassion;

second: he must make sacrifice for himself.

The first is a result that honours his ministry, the second is a result that dishonours his ministry -.

1. The Cause of His Honour

Here is the honour of a High Priest taken from other men: "he knows how to be compassionate toward the wayward and the ignorant."

Concerning this, Barclay says,

> "The priest must be a man; he must be completely involved in the human situation; he must be bound up with men in the bundle of life; he must live with them and feel with them and know their heights and their depths. In connection with this (the apostle) used a wonderful word - the word `metriopathein'. It may be translated `to feel gently', although it is really one of those untranslatable Greek words. The Greeks always defined a virtue as the mean between two extremes. On either hand there was an extreme into which a man might fall; in between there was the right thing and the right way. Virtue to the Greek was a balance of mean, the right point between two extremes. So the Greeks defined `metriopatheia' as the mean between extravagant grief and utter indifference. It was feeling about men in the right way, `the mid-course between explosions of anger and lazy indulgence'. It is that sympathetic feeling which enabled a man to raise up and to save, to spare and to hear. Men lack this feeling when they refuse to be reconciled with someone who has differed from them. It means the ability to bear with people without getting irritated and annoyed; it means the ability not to lose one's temper with people when they are foolish and when they will not learn and when they do the same thing over and over again and when they seem to be senselessly blind. It describes the attitude to others which does not issue in anger at the fault and which does not condone the fault, but which to the end of the day spends itself in a gentle yet powerful sympathy, which by its very patience moulds a man back on to the right way. No man can ever deal with his fellow-men unless

he has this strong and patient, this God-given `metriopatheia` - `compassion`.[19]

2.   The Cause of His Dishonour

The dishonour of a high priest taken from other men lies in this: he too experiences many infirmities. Therefore he must offer sacrifice, not only for the sins of the people, but also for his own sins.

At once the apostle can show the contrast between Christ and Aaron. Like every other human high priest, Aaron was unavoidably a sinner. But Christ was given to us, not taken from among us; therefore he alone had no need to offer sacrifice for any personal sin.

C. APPOINTED BY COMMAND OF GOD

A priest must be a person appointed by God. No one can take this office by his own choice. It is not a profession, nor a means of employment or of gaining wealth. It is a privilege, a calling of God. A true priest is a man chosen by the Lord for the greatest privilege that can be bestowed -

> *"No one can take this honour of his own accord; it belongs only to those, like Aaron, who are called to the office by God"[20]*

Aaron was the man who most nearly fulfilled the ideal of a true high priest. But he failed, as did all who came after him. One Priest alone has succeeded, as the apostle now shows -

THE CHARACTERISTICS OF CHRIST

See He 5:5-10. As we have seen, the ideal high priest is

- chosen by God
- compassionate toward others
- consecrated to offer sacrifice.

Many have nearly fulfilled that ideal; yet in the end every human priest fails because of personal sin. But the apostle, having earlier declared that

---

[19] The Daily Study Bible, William Barclay; Saint Andrew Press, Edinburgh, 1959; "The letter to the Hebrews", pg 44,45. Abridged and slightly altered.

[20] He 5:4; Ex 28:1-3; Nu 16:1-40.

Christ was a man truly without sin, now shows that he also bears the three other characteristics of true priesthood -

A. CHRIST WAS CHOSEN BY GOD (vs. 5-6)

"Christ did not try to exalt himself by seizing the office of High Priest."

He did not arrogate to himself that calling; he is High Priest by the authority of God, who said to him, *"You are my Son, and today I have become your Father!"* (vs. 5) The saying comes from Psalm 2:7 and the apostle has quoted it before (1:5) to prove the deity of Christ. Since he was already Son of God, no further glory could accrue to him from becoming High Priest. This new office brought him no gain; he did not accept it for his own benefit. Therefore, he must have done so for our benefit. How astonishing is the grace of the Father. Just for our glory God placed his Son as our High Priest in the heavenly Tabernacle.

This high calling and superior position of Christ stands confirmed by another quote: *"You are a priest for ever after the order of Melchizedek"* - which comes from Psalm 110:4. There also the psalmist says that Christ's high office is attested by solemn oath, "The Lord has sworn and will not change his mind ... " So the oracles declared that Christ would be a Priest, and that he would be a Priest for ever.

B. CHRIST IS COMPASSIONATE TOWARD US (vs. 7-8)

Though he was the Son of God and had eternally existed with God, for the sake of establishing an everlasting High Priesthood he became a man. For a "short time" he had a body of flesh. Out of this sharing in our humanity grew his capacity to be compassionate toward us. Notice how the apostle highlights the human dimension of Christ -

1. Jesus was dependent upon prayer

"When he was on earth, Jesus offered up prayers and supplications."

Here is an offering that is acceptable to God. It is an offering that anyone may make. It consists of "prayers" and "supplications" -

(a) "Prayer" is earnestly asking God for some desired blessing". It includes offering to God adoration, thanksgiving, and devotion. The word used in the text specifically means "petition", that is, making a request to God, particularly a formal request for some right or privilege to be fulfilled. It is a request soliciting some special action, or grant; an appeal to the justice and mercy of God. Jesus prayed this way, as perfect Man, and knew that his Father would give him his request. So may we, in Christ, also pray.

(b) "Supplication" is a passionate, fervent, craving for some desperately needed help. Jesus called this kind of prayer "importunate" - as when a person implores God for urgent assistance; or as when Peter shrieked "Lord, save me!" (Mt 14:30). It is passionate pleading and earnest entreaty. It is praying from the heat of an intense craving. It is a powerful crying to God that breaks down every barrier and violently impels itself to the throne of the Deity. Supplication is praying that takes heaven by force (Mt 11:12). When Jesus made supplications to his Father, he prayed with "passionate cries and tears" - a phrase that expresses profound emotion, trenchant desire, urgent need.

The word "crying" in the original stems from an ancient root meaning to "croak" (as a raven) - an awful strangled sound, symbolic of horror. The Greeks used the word to describe the

- screech of a person terrified by some fearful apparition
- desperate cry of a drowning man to a passerby
- spirited plea of a person opposing a death penalty
- dire lamentation of a bereaved mother.

The word also expresses the forcible outcry of a mob against a criminal, the boisterous clamour of a crowd demanding some right, and the like. Jesus offered up such prayers. Sometimes he called upon God with cries of earnest entreaty; at other times he petitioned as a man insisting upon his legal rights. He was familiar also with fervent supplications, the "passionate cries and tears" of a man who has a desperate need. In this he set us an example; and, as one who is fellow to us, he also established his right to speak for us.

2. *Jesus was heard when he prayed*

In the stark words of the old version, "He was heard, because he feared!"

Jesus was heard because he prayed; he prayed because he expected to be heard. Jesus was heard because he feared; he feared because he knew he was heard. He was therefore careful to speak nothing rash. He feared that without prayer he would fail. He had a dread of being held in the chains of death, and therefore prayed to "God who was able to deliver him from death" by keeping him on the path of righteousness. Death was therefore unable to hold him.

More particularly, the word "fear" means here:

- he was heard because of his reverence in worship
- he was heard because of his piety of conduct
- he was heard because of his hatred of sin
- he was heard because of his caution in speaking
- he was heard because of his circumspection in action.

Here too the Lord has set us an example in prayer. For this reason he is able to be compassionate toward us when by weakness we fall short of this example. He is especially willing to show compassion to those who follow his example. They, like him, will be heard, because they fear.

3.   *Jesus had to learn obedience*

> *"Although he was a Son, he still had to learn obedience*
> *by the things that he suffered" (vs. 8).*

Was Jesus then disobedient to the Father? Not at all. On the contrary, he was entirely without sin. But before he could establish a true and eternal High Priesthood he had to taste the experience of being made "obedient". See the enlargement of this in Ph 2:5-8 -

"Though he was the Son"	"Since Christ possessed the form of God, it was not arrogance for him to claim equality with God
"Yet he had to learn obedience"	"Yet he freely discarded all honour, and assuming the form of a slave, taking on human likeness and becoming a man."
"By the things that he suffered"	"He humbled himself, and became obedient to the point of death, even to dying on a cross"

So Jesus grew in knowledge. He discovered first-hand the burdens suffered by men and women; he acquired experience in human problems;

he "learned" from his companions those things that are simple, and those that are difficult. In thus learning obedience, the Lord established the habit of always implicitly obeying God. He complied with every word of his Father; he grew in hatred of sin and love of righteousness; he kept every law prescribed in the Scripture; he tasted mankind's deepest joys and bitterest griefs. In all these things he was "made perfect" - that is, he became thoroughly suited to the office of High Priest; he carried out fully the purpose for which he had come.

C. CHRIST WAS CONSECRATED BY GOD (vs. 9-10)

This is the third characteristic of the ideal High Priest. Jesus entirely satisfied this demand in his personal sacrifice on the cross.

> *"Once he had been made perfect, then he became the source of eternal salvation to everyone who obeys him, and God has named him High Priest for ever after the order of Melchizedek." (He 5:9-10)*

He is the "source". The Greek word occurs only here. It means literally that Christ is the "causative" of eternal salvation. Salvation springs entirely from him. Apart from him we would have for ever hunted for it in vain. Christ himself was the Designer of our salvation, and the means of its provision stem from him alone. It was he who produced its law, who formed its pattern in the Tabernacle, who first moved in its operation. Through his labour it was born, in his tears it was sanctified, by his strong crying it was accepted by God, in his obedient suffering it was made effective for all mankind.

He is the author of *"eternal salvation"*. Not such salvation as the high priests of old secured, which merely lasted from one sacrifice to the next, and was often forgotten, and the sacrifices often omitted. This salvation of Christ is eternal. It will never be taken from the believer by God. Our great High Priest will never fail in his intercession, nor ever withdraw his sacrifice, nor will his grace ever lose its efficacy.

"Salvation" here implies "rescue into a place of perfect safety". Human rescue often means "out of the frying pan, into the fire". Not so with this salvation. And what is this "rescue"? It means being

- rescued from the confinement of the world and brought into the expansiveness and brilliance of heaven

- rescued from the violence of Satan who goes around like a *"roaring lion, seeking whom he may devour"*
- rescued from the danger of being cast into the lake of fire, and brought instead into the mansions of God
- rescued from the restraint of the flesh and entering into the liberty of the Spirit
- rescued from being exposed to evil and entering instead into the influence of righteousness
- rescued from the kingdom of darkness and coming into the kingdom of God's dear Son.

This is indeed a great rescue! This is indeed a wonderful safety!

Note though: it is contingent upon *"obedience"*; for it belongs only to those who "obey him". Do you want to benefit from this splendid rescue? Then listen attentively to the words of Christ, pay careful heed to the way of Christ, and diligently conform to the will of Christ. An obedient person is one who is

- submissive to the purpose of the Lord
- complies with the commands of the Lord
- follows the direction of the Lord
- acts on the injunctions of the Lord
- subject to the rule of the Lord
- governed by the authority of the Lord
- yields to the influence of the Lord
- acknowledges the control of the Lord

Only in such obedience can each believer find perfect safety. To fall short of it leads to neglect of this salvation, and *"how can we escape if we neglect this great salvation?"* (He 2:3). However, let us take comfort in the knowledge that in all these things Christ was perfect, and perfectly conformed to the pattern of a true High Priest. For this cause scripture pronounces him *"High Priest for ever"*. Therefore we may *"come boldly to the throne of grace, and there obtain mercy, and find grace to help in time of need."* What folly it would be for any to turn back from such a Priest, to return to the old order and its imperfections. What wrath such an insult to God must deserve. Heed the urgent warning of the apostle: "Stay you faltering Hebrews; hold fast to your faith in Christ, for in him alone lies eternal salvation!"

CHAPTER SIX:

MELCHIZEDEK

Text: Hebrews 7:1-22

The apostle wants to demonstrate the excellency of Christ's priesthood, and to show its impact upon the new and better covenant God has made with us. Before he can do this, he must prove that Jesus is superior to the line of Aaron. Is that impossible? No, for he simply goes back to Abraham and shows how Abraham was less than Christ. How can he do that? He uses the story of Melchizedek, to whom Abraham paid tithes.

At once we find ourselves among those things that he said earlier are "strong meat" and "difficult to understand" -

> *"There are many things I must tell you about Melchizedek, but because you are such dullards you may find them too hard to grasp ... I want to give you `meat' but find instead that I must keep feeding you `milk'. You are just like suckling babies, who are not yet old enough to know right from wrong. You should instead be `adults', long accustomed to separating good and evil, and so able to receive solid food!" (He 5:11-14).*

I hope that you, dear reader, will fare better, as we consider

THE MYSTERY OF MELCHIZEDEK

Apart from our leading text (He 7:1-22), this strange priest is mentioned in the following places: Ge 14:18-20; Ps 110:4; He 5:6,10,11; 6:20. From those accounts we learn that -

A. KING OF SALEM

Melchizedek was the king of Salem, an ancient name for the city of Jerusalem. He was also "the priest of the Most High God" Notice the definite article. He was not merely one of many priests, but singularly appointed by the Lord. Perhaps we are meant to conclude that he was the only priest who still served God. All the others had turned to idolatry. Melchizedek refused to follow them, and remained a monotheistic priest.

Despite the prevailing lawlessness that was choking the knowledge of God out of Palestine, it seems that a little group of God-fearing people clustered in Salem around this Royal Priest. Under his guidance they worshipped the Lord with a devout and sincere faith.

But was he more than just a priest-king?

1.   A Supernatural Man?

Some writers suggest that Melchizedek was the Lord Jesus Christ. He was, they say, a "Christophany" - an appearance of Christ upon the earth before his actual incarnation. Here are some of their reasons -

(a) Can anyone described as Melchizedek was be just an ordinary man? He lacked (we are told) father, mother, and all ancestry; and he had neither beginning of days nor end of life.

(b) He "brought out" (created?) bread and wine to give to Abraham, which is symbolic of the sacrament of the Lord's Supper.

(c) Scripture never refers to his personal existence in the past tense. The word "was" (Ge 14:18; He 7:4) is in italics; it is not in the original. Every verb in the original referring to his person is in the present tense.

(d) He 7:8 says, "scripture affirms that he is alive"; that is, Melchizedek did not die, which could only be true of Christ.

(e) "King of Righteousness" is a title that belongs only to God, and to his Righteous Servant" (Is 53:11); that is, to Christ, who came to establish righteousness on the earth.

(f) Can any other mere man stand higher than Abraham in the favour of God? Therefore Melchizedek must have been more than man.

2.   A Natural Man

There is strength in some of those arguments. Nonetheless, it still seems more reasonable (and scriptural) to suppose that Melchizedek was an ordinary man. He was simply the King of Salem, and the appointed priest of his people. Why this is so will become clearer as we move along.

3.   A Picture of Christ

(a) Melchizedek "brought out" bread and wine (Ge 14:18). The phrase may mean "created", but there is no reason to claim that it must do so. The same word is used many times in the OT in a great variety of ways: break out, bear, carry out, go abroad, depart, escape, fall, grow, proceed, etc.

Although Hebrews does not mention the meal provided by Melchizedek, we are probably right to see in it a further similarity between him and Christ. The "bread and wine" powerfully symbolise the elements of the Lord's Supper.

(b) Melchizedek was "priest of the most high God". In Hebrew, this is "El Elyon", - the "Almighty", the "Highest". It is first used in scripture in this place, which also attaches its most significant meaning: "the Creator of heaven and earth." So powerful was the impact made upon Abraham by this revelation of God, he at once gave a tithe of all he had to Melchizedek. See how reverently Abraham used this new name of God for the first time. Mark the profound impression it had made upon him -

> *"The king of Sodom said to Abraham, `Give my people back to me, and you can keep the rest of the plunder for yourself.' But Abraham replied, `I raised my hand and swore to the Lord, the <u>Most High God, the Creator of heaven and earth</u>, that I will not take from you so much as a thread or shoe lace" (Ge 14:21-23)*

God is "Most High". There is none higher than he in majesty or perfection. Before his holiness, wisdom, strength, and splendour all other strength becomes feeble, all other light turns dark. Surely this must constrain us to humility and reverence: God is great and we are small, except in one thing: whom the Lord God honours is honoured indeed! Therefore among priests who can stand higher than he whom the Almighty has appointed to the sacred office?

God is Creator of heaven and earth. To him alone belongs the right to partition the nations (De 32:8), to form the earth, to rule the angels, to determine the destiny of all things. His authority is supreme, both in heaven and on earth. He alone occupies the height and the depth, the length and the breadth of all things. The Lord has all realms entirely in his power, nor can any wrest them from his grasp. By unchallenged right he owns heaven and earth. By undeniable prerogative he seeks enjoyment from them. He alone deserves to be known as their master, to gain their treasure, to receive their praise.

Because he is Sovereign, he is able to distribute privilege, responsibility, and calling to whom he will. His patent to order all things to his own pleasure and advantage is incontestable. It is the proper duty of men and women to make themselves suitable to God's purpose, useful in God's calling.

(c) Melchizedek blessed Abraham because of God; and blessed God because of Abraham. Abraham found blessing because, when he gave tithes to God, he became possessor of a God who possessed all. What need had he then of the wealth of a Sodomite king? And blessing accrued to God because of the massive victory his hand had wrought for Abraham. May not the owner of an object dispose of it in any way he chooses? The Lord God, being owner of all, was easily able to deliver Abraham's enemies into his hand. Even that arch enemy Satan is subject to the Almighty, who will do with him whatever he pleases. By faith, we may move the Lord to behave toward us as he did to Abraham.

(d) Abraham gave tithes to Melchizedek, a surprising action that unknowingly fore-shadowed the dissolution of the levitical priesthood. It also provided a theme for the psalmist, who looked back on the ancient drama and saw in it a vision of the new priesthood. He spoke in wonder about the integration of the office of priest and king in one person -

> *"The Lord has sworn and will never change his mind,*
> *`You are a priest for ever after the order of Melchizedek*
> *... From Zion you will reign over all your enemies'" (Ps*
> *110:4,2).*

Here is a priesthood established by an explicit oath of God. How then can it fail? A pledge so authorised none can ever revoke, which makes this priesthood so different from all others. They all suffer severe fluctuation from nobility to debasement, from honour to shame, from life to death -

> *"This is what the Lord God of Israel says: `Once I*
> *promised that the house of you and your descendants*
> *would be my priests for all time;' but that is his word no*
> *longer. This is what he now says: `I can no longer*
> *tolerate you. Those who honour me I will honour; and*
> *those who despise me will be despised" (1 Sa 2:30).*

Melchizedek was not such a priest. He placed great honour upon God, and so was honoured by God. Even Abraham was compelled to acknowledge his superiority. Therefore the Lord decided to make him the supreme type of the Royal and eternal High-Priestly ministry of his Son.

Psalm 110 speaks entirely of the Lord Jesus Christ[21], foretelling his message as Prophet, his ministry as Priest, and his monarchy as Prince. Even the Jews acknowledged that the Psalm spoke of the Messiah. When Jesus questioned the Pharisees on the first words of the Psalm, they chose to say nothing rather than deny the very evident truth of what he had said. Unable to refute his argument, they had to submit to disgrace (Mt 22:41-46). The Psalm clearly predicted that the Messiah would come, that he would be the Son of God, and that he would establish an eternal priesthood protected by the sworn oath of God.

B. PRIEST OF GOD

We come now to the NT references to Melchizedek -

1.   The first is Hebrews 5:6.

Here the apostle begins to show how the priesthood of Christ locks into the order of Melchizedek. Two things are important here -

a   the revelation of Christ as the Son of God.

Note verse 5, "You are my Son". His priesthood does not depend upon a lineal descent from Levi, but from the parentage of the Father. Therefore he is a priest apart from Aaron, and divorced from the rites and rituals of the Temple.

b.   the resurrection of Christ as the Saviour of the world.

"On this day I became your Father." The resurrection sealed the sinlessness of Christ. It also demonstrated his absolute right to be Universal Priest and his perfect qualifications for that high office (cp. Ro 1:4).

His resurrection sealed Christ as the anti-type of Melchizedek. This was unconsciously pre-figured by Melchizedek, when he set a meal before Abraham. As I have said above, a Christian cannot mistake the

---

[21] See Mt 22:44; Ac 2:34; etc.

symbolism of bread and wine. They irresistibly remind us of the sacrifice and the resurrection of our Lord.

If Christ is both Son and Saviour, then his office of high priest can have no ending. So the Father says, "You are a priest for ever." He is thus able to be "the originator of eternal salvation for all who obey him" (vs. 9).

2. *The second is Hebrews 5:10*

> *"God has declared that you are High Priest for ever, after the order of Melchizedek."*

Christ's calling resulted from his perfection: "After he was perfect ... he was called" (vs. 9,10) Our perfection results from our calling. Christ, having learned what obedience means, is now able to succour those who have disobeyed, and save those who do obey. Further, since he is the Author of Salvation, God has decreed that he shall also be the Administrator of it. God has chosen him to be the only High Priest, and commands all men so to acknowledge him.

Now Christ was perfected and consecrated to the office of High Priest by his sorrow (He 5:7-8). His blood is the dye that colours his sacerdotal robes. Since he was willing to suffer to secure the office of High Priest, the Saviour will not fail to serve in that office. So he is called a High Priest "after the order of Melchizedek." We will have more to say about this, but note here:

- respecting work, Christ fulfils the function of the Aaronic priesthood; but,
- respecting office, he stands in the room of Melchizedek.

What does the "order of Melchizedek" mean? We could suggest that it entails -

- a royal authority like that of Melchizedek the Priest-King
- an endless life, after the pattern of Melchizedek, who is said to have neither beginning nor ending
- the character of Melchizedek, who was a "King of Righteousness" and a "King of Peace".
- a divine appointment like that of Melchizedek, apart from the human descent upon which the Aaronic priests were dependent.

3. The third is Hebrews 6:20.

"Like a forerunner, Jesus has gone into the heavenly sanctuary ahead of us, where he has become High Priest for ever after the order of Melchizedek."

The word "forerunner" occurs only here. It means a "scout", "pioneer", or "trail-blazer". It shows that he has gone before us to prepare the way, to provide a place for us where he is, and to give us assurance that we will surely follow him. Where has he gone? "Within the veil." Why did he go there? Just "for us". He is there for our benefit and happiness, to provide us with hope.

After he entered the holiest, Jesus "was made High Priest for ever". He earned this noble title because he was the forerunner of all the redeemed of all ages. Having travelled the gamut of human experience, he alone was sufficient for the task. Having now entered, he will never leave until he has entirely accomplished his task of priestly ministry. And what is that task? Simply to ensure that his people inherit the promises. So did Melchizedek bless Abraham, and so is Christ a priest for ever after the order of Melchizedek.

See the certainty of this stupendous ministry of the Lord, expressed by the apostle in three imperatives -

- "You are a priest for ever after the order of Melchizedek"
- "Called by God High Priest after the order of Melchizedek."
- "Made High Priest for ever after the order of Melchizedek."

Because Christ was born as a Son, he was destined to be priest. Because he was obedient as a Son, he was designated High Priest. Because he triumphed as the Son, he was declared High Priest for ever!

Upon Christ, therefore, we must lock all our hope of happiness. To him we may flee for strong consolation. He is a sure refuge and a steadfast anchor. By him we shall reach heaven, and in him find eternal safety and satisfaction.

All this - because Jesus is made "High Priest for ever after the order of Melchizedek."

THE MAJESTY OF MELCHIZEDEK

"You should mark how great this man was. Even the patriarch Abraham gave him a tithe of all the plunder ... Melchizedek, King of Salem and Priest of the Most High God, met Abraham when he was returning from his triumph over the allied kings. Melchizedek blessed Abraham, and the patriarch gave him a tithe of his booty" (He 7:1-2,4).

With remarkable insight, the apostle demonstrates the superiority of Jesus to Abraham by showing the inferiority of Abraham to Melchizedek. Why does he find this necessary? Because the Aaronic priesthood, which stemmed from Abraham, had failed, and God had to repair the damage. But how will God do this? There are three possibilities: mend the old priesthood; establish a new one; go back to a more primitive model. The latter became God's choice. The apostle argues that far from the priesthood of Jesus being invalidated because he did not belong to the clan of Levi, his claim rested upon an even stronger foundation. He reached back past Aaron, even past Abraham, to achieve the restoration of the original divine office of priest-king. He linked himself with the Order of Melchizedek - to whom even Abraham had offered obeisance.

The purpose of priesthood is to offer a sufficient sacrifice for sin, and to provide people with a means of access to God. In both ways the priests of Israel failed. How? Because the Law that was meant to provide a way into the presence of God had instead become a rod of death. So, although the sacrifices lay constantly upon the altar, the hearts of the worshippers remained heavy with the guilt of sin; the atonement they hoped for remained elusive.

Even the Lord himself had said,

"What's the use of your endless sacrifices? They are worthless to me. I am sick of your burnt offerings of rams, and of the fat of your fat animals. Do you really think I find any pleasure in the blood of bullocks, or in the slaughter of lambs and goats?" (Is 1:11).

How startling such words must have sounded to a people accustomed to thinking that God himself had ordained their sacrifices! Yet the prophet simply stated the obvious: the death of a brute beast could hardly atone for the sins of a rational man. But now the Lord has established in Christ a new priesthood, with an acceptable sacrifice, a sure access, a true satisfaction.

This benefit, however, belongs only to those who obey him. How? By abandoning animal immolations and an earthly priesthood. Do you want a door to heaven? Then you must come by way of the greater priesthood of Christ, whose office Abraham showed was superior when he gave homage to Melchizedek. Nor should this seem strange. Did not the psalmist long ago foretell that such a priesthood would arise? So the apostle now shows how radically different from the old order is the new, and how high Christ stands above Aaron. He illustrates this by the showing the greatness of Melchizedek -

A. MELCHIZEDEK WAS A KING

In the ordinary sense, Melchizedek was just a man who happened to be king over the other inhabitants of the land. But scripture gives a typical significance both to his name and his realm (vs 2).

His name was Melchizedek, which is "The King of Righteousness. His realm was Salem, which means he was "The King of Peace". Notice how carefully those two are placed: "first" righteousness, "after that" peace. There can be no peace without righteousness. Always in scripture righteousness takes precedence over peace (Ps 85:10) -

> "The work of righteousness shall be peace; and the effect of righteousness quietness and assurance for ever" (Is 32 :17, KJV) ... "If we are (first) justified by faith, then we shall (second) have peace with God" (Ro 5:1)... "The kingdom of God (begins with) righteousness, (then follow) peace and joy" (Ro 14:7).

So Melchizedek is called king before he is named priest. From this we learn again that only those can find Christ as Priest who first acknowledge him as King. There can be no compromise here, no lessening of this standard. In the purpose of God, Melchizedek did not meet Abraham until he was "returning from his triumph over the allied kings". That is, only after he found Abraham engaged in a righteous work did the Lord see to it that he received blessing and peace.

Likewise, the first righteous work God requires of us is repentance. He must find us turning from the land of the enemy and facing toward the heavenly Jerusalem, the city of eternal peace. Then we should also engage in the warfare of faith, resisting the enemies of God and upholding the honour of the Lord. Do such things and you will be able to meet the true Melchizedek without fear. You will receive from him the living bread, the water of life, the unending blessing of heaven.

Make Christ the Lord of Righteousness in your life; then he will unfailingly be also the Prince of Peace. Those two noble titles, which demonstrably lift the order of Melchizedek far above the Aaronic order, will describe your relationship with the Saviour. By contrast, the levitical priests held a much lower rank:

- they were forbidden to accept a royal crown
- because of unrighteousness they had to offer sacrifice for their own sins, as well as those of the people
- they were unable by their ministry to bring lasting peace to the hearts of the people
- year by year the repeating sacrifices testified to their own inadequacy.

Not so Melchizedek. He was ordained both priest and king, and even Abraham was content to pay him tithes.

B. MELCHIZEDEK WAS A PRIEST

Standing alone, splendid, dignified, mysterious; solitary priest of the Most High God - what glory rests upon him! The one faithful witness of the Almighty in a world lying in heavy darkness; the one brilliant star in a black sky. The Bible records no other priest like Melchizedek. His was a priesthood characterised by

- righteousness
- peace
- royal birth
- continuance
- divine calling.

A priesthood such as this is truly fit to be taken up, filled, and immeasurably exalted by the Son of God.

How Jesus does this is the theme of the next chapter.

CHAPTER SEVEN:

EVERLASTING

text: Hebrews 7:1-22 (cont.)

Melchizedek held the title "Priest of the Most High God, which at once separates him from the family of Aaron. Their priesthood depended upon the agreement God had made with Israel under the name "Yahweh" - "Lord of the Covenant" - and they held the title "Servants of Yahweh". But Melchizedek served at the altar of El Elyon - "The Most High God" - a glorious name whose universal sweep embraced both heaven and earth, angels and all mankind. By contrast, "Yahweh" belonged particularly to the covenant God had made with Israel; it was linked with the priestly rights of just one family. El Elyon scorned any national restriction. It expressed the rule of God over all peoples; it reached back to the more ancient covenant God had made with all the families of the earth; it embraced his world-wide benevolence.

How great then was the privilege this old priest-king enjoyed! The God before whom he ministered governed from the lofty heights of glory but kept his eye also on the smallest sparrow. Monarch of every realm, Father of every race, enormously powerful yet boundless in mercy, this Most High God created the order of Melchizedek. Can you doubt that its priest stood higher than Aaron? The apostle was sure of it -

AN IMPERISHABLE PRIESTHOOD

A. MELCHIZEDEK WAS PRIEST BY PERSONAL RIGHT

"Without father or mother, without lineage, showing neither beginning of days, nor end of life" (7:3).

Do those words prove that Melchizedek was actually Christ? Probably not, for the very next sentence says that he was only "like the Son of God." It would be strange also to make Christ a type of himself. More likely, the apostle simply recognised that the hand of the Holy Spirit had shaped the brief record of Melchizedek. By omitting all details about his birth or death the Spirit turned Melchizedek into a figure of Christ. Remember also that Genesis abounds in genealogies, which makes this sudden appearance of Melchizedek unusual. Normally, particular care was given to establishing the correct lineage for a priest. For example, every Jewish priest had to produce a genealogy traced back to Jacob's son Levi. The law banned from office any priest who lacked proof of his levitical lineage (see Ezra 2:62-63; Ex 29:9,29-30; Le 21:13-14; etc.).

What then did the priesthood of Melchizedek depend on? It was not by right of natural descent. Therefore it must have been by right of personal qualification. His was not a legal, but a personal calling. A priest in Israel's Temple was ordained because his father had been priest before him, and his son would be priest after him. But Melchizedek inherited his office from none, nor could he pass it on to any.

Supremely the Lord Jesus Christ is the perfect fulfilment of this pattern. He is priest solely by personal right and achievement; not by inheritance, not by law, but declared so by the will of God, and made so by the command of God.

B. MELCHIZEDEK WAS "MADE LIKE THE SON OF GOD"

The apostle argues that Melchizedek was only a type, chosen by the Spirit to pre-figure Christ. Now it is interesting to notice the words used to describe his eternity and his personal right -

1. *"Without lineage"*

This is one of the many vivid words that are peculiar to Hebrews. Barclay says this is the first recorded use of the word. No record exists of any Greek writer using it before this time, which suggests that the apostle created it just for this letter. He wanted to show that Christ's priesthood does not depend upon human descent, but solely upon divine choice.

2. *"Without father or mother"*

The Greeks used this phrase to describe run away children, or children of loose birth, whose parents either could not be found, or were unknown. Used in contempt, spoken as an insult, the words "without father or mother" isolated the victim from society. Applied to Christ, they show his solitary splendour: he depends upon no other for his honour; he holds it by personal right alone.

3.   Melchizedek "remains a priest for ever"

That is, being made a type of Christ, Melchizedek becomes an heir to the salvation of Christ. Therefore the promise made by Christ belongs to him also: "They will be priests and kings to God" (Re 1:6).

Since there is no record of his birth or of his death, he becomes a perfect type of God's supreme High Priest. He prefigures the Son of God, who was before the beginning and who will go on beyond the end. Once again the Aaronic priesthood stands surpassed: that was local, temporary, national; this is universal, international, eternal.

Melchizedek is the first man named in scripture as "cohen" (priest), and the only one recorded as carrying this office in the name of Righteousness, Peace, and the Most High God. Therefore he is a fine type of the Son of God who has established this priesthood anew, never to be disbanded.

What hope it inspires in the trembling heart to hear the constant echo of the words, "You are Priest for ever". Repeatedly the eternity of his office commands our attention. Looking at Jesus, we discover two things irrevocably rooted in his nature: sacrifice and priesthood. Those qualities have for ages past distinguished the Son of God, and will for ages yet to come. For this cause, the Saviour can never desert the high office to which he is called by God. Nor will he ever fail to show compassion, and to be merciful and gracious.

See the witness of the eternal nature of the Saviour's priesthood -

- "He remains a priest for ever" (vs. 3)
- "Scripture affirms that he is ever-living" (vs. 8)
- "His priesthood depends upon the power of an endless life" (vs. 16)
- "You are a priest for ever" (vs. 21)
- "He lives for ever" (vs. 24)
- "He has an unalterable priesthood" (vs. 24)
- "He is always there to make intercession" (vs. 25)
- "He is consecrated for ever" (vs. 28)

4. _Melchizedek accepted tithes from Levi_

- see verses 4-10.

(a) Abraham, the father of Israel, gave a tithe to Melchizedek and received blessing from him. Therefore the office of this Priest-King is higher than the patriarch's. It takes precedence even over the nation (Israel) that stemmed from Abraham.

(b) The Levites received tithes from their own people. But Melchizedek took them from a stranger. Although he was a Gentile ruler, he claimed tithes from Abraham the Hebrew. Nevertheless, the Levites held a high honour: they "received the office of priesthood ... were instructed to take tithes from their brothers ... according to the law ... and were descended from Abraham, the man who received the promises." Those things, put together, comprise an exalted office, one that seems impossible to surpass.

Yet Melchizedek bore a greater honour:

- they received the office, but he was made a priest
- they received tithes by law, he received them by personal right
- they acted by commandment, he ministered through love
- they were descended from Abraham, who himself bowed before Melchizedek.

Though Abraham had received promises from God, Melchizedek received a greater promise. How else could he hold the right to bless Abraham? Further, the very existence of the levitical priesthood depended upon death and succession. Scripture tells of their death; but it speaks of Melchizedek as if he were always alive.

(c) Notice here how one generation is responsible to another. Generations of Levites are said to have been bound to the action of Abraham -

> "You could even say that Levi, who had a right to collect tithes, actually paid tithes through his ancestor Abraham. Was he not still in Abraham's body when the patriarch met Melchizedek?"

Our actions pass to our posterity, whether for good or evil. That is how the whole race incurred the guilt of Adam's transgression. We were in Adam when he sinned, and the depravity that passed into him then passes upon us now. That is why any hope we have of gaining salvation rests entirely upon the grace of God.

(d)   Melchizedek, we are told, was *"made like the Son of God,"* which was never said of Levi.   Therefore the apostle concludes that Christ must be superior to the levitical order of priests. That order has run its appointed course; succour can now be found in Christ alone.

AN IMPERFECT PRIESTHOOD

- see Hebrews 7:11-19

A. AN IMPERMANENT PRIESTHOOD (vs. 11-12)

The levitical priesthood did possess greatness, for under it the people received the law of God. Yet therein lay its very weakness. The law was designed to bring people to God, to enable them to have fellowship with him. But they could not keep it.   Human folly made ritual sacrifices necessary to atone for disobedience to the law. Those sacrifices could cover sin, but they were quite incapable of giving any victory over it. So the entire apparatus became a "ministry of death" (2 Co 3:7).

Therefore a new priesthood had to be established on a new principle. The Law and the Levites were so bound together that to abolish the one was to abolish the other. The order of Aaron had failed; so Christ raised again in himself the order of Melchizedek. Inevitably, the displacement of the Levites cause the annulling of the Law, so that now we must approach God by way of his new law - the gospel.

B. A NEW ORDER ARISES (vs. 13-15)

The priesthood now arises from an entirely different tribe. Like Melchizedek, who was a gentile, Christ ("of whom these things are spoken") did not belong to the priestly family. He came from the tribe of Judah. But the law of Moses forbade anyone from that tribe to "serve at the altar". Therefore God had to establish a new altar with a changed sacrifice. That is why the prophet said that God's anointed priest, when he came, would not be of the order of Aaron, but would be "patterned upon Melchizedek".

1. The Perfection of the New Order (vs. 16,17)

The Levites were ordained to office under "a set of rules that required a correct lineage". Notice here -

(a) The law governing levitical office had to deal with their frailty, sinfulness, and humanity. It made provision for their death, and the descent of the office from father to son. Here then is the imperfection of all human priesthood. The troubled sinner may find a good priest, one with compassion and wisdom; but soon this good man must die, and then where will the bereft soul turn for help? A priesthood confined within death and succession could not possibly convey lasting blessing to its patron.

(b) The law governing levitical office consisted of a mass of ritual. Its detailed rules dealt with physical things, such as sundry washings, minute observances, and the like. But it did not really touch the worshippers' souls, nor quicken their spirits. People would (and did) die for the sake of the law. Yet it remained "carnal", centred on the "body". It always touched those things that were outward more than those that were inner.

By contrast, Christ's consecration to priesthood was made in "the power of an endless life". What is that power? What is that life? The apostle means the tremendous power Christ has both to sustain life within himself and to communicate that life to those who trust him. He said of himself -

> "I will lay down my life, so that I may take it up again.
> No one can take it from me; I will lay it down by myself.
> I have power to lay it down, and I have power to take it
> up again. The Father himself gave me that instruction"
> (Jn 10:17-18).

Those who believe in Christ receive not only eternal life, and with it the power of that life: power that can destroy death and abolish the cause of death - sin.

So then, Christ stands for ever as priest, not by some ephemeral rule, but by the unshakeable strength of God. By this immutable decree the Father founded the priestly office of the Son: "You are a priest for ever!" So his ministry can never change, for it does not depend upon earthly observance, but upon spiritual might. It does not minister death, but life -

eternal life, powerful life. At the altar of Christ the sinner will always find sufficient grace, ever present help, and deep mercy. The life that waits there is indestructible and permanent - it can be lost only if it is wilfully cast away.

2. The Failure of the Law (vs. 18,19)

Nothing more clearly shows that the law "made nothing perfect" than the endless sacrifices the priests offered on Israel's altars. The nation's unchanging imperfection proved the futility of animal immolation. Therefore the apostle indicted the levitical system in two stern words. He says that it was

3. Weak

That is, "strengthless". The law remained impotent in the face of deepest human need. The severity of sin rose beyond its ability to save. Exhaustion quickly overcame its promise of deliverance. Because it was too flimsy to lift a sinner from the slough of degradation, therefore it could not help people to withstand the onslaught of evil, nor was it able to unite many nations under the one faith. Though it held a promise of righteousness, it wanted in ability to perform that promise. Power-less in operation, inefficient in activity, it was feeble because it had no real life, no true energy to impart. It could neither prevail to break down sin nor to build up righteousness.

4. Unprofitable

That is, the law did not produce the end it proposed. It was fruitless in its results, ineffectual in its methods. Inherent within the law were difficulties and weaknesses that forbade it any hope of real success. The law therefore became unserviceable, and left only one recourse: abolish it and produce a better principle. Therefore it was annulled, and rendered legally void (2 Co 3:7-11). Since it had no further use, God abolished it by an irreversible decree.

How foolish, then, for anyone to restore any of the provisions of the ancient law, as if by keeping some of its rules we can gain an advantage beyond what Christ gives. Especially sad are those pastors who want to re-establish in themselves a sacerdotal ministry. They pronounce themselves mediators between God and the people. They claim to offer sacrifice anew in the Eucharist, turning the Table of Christ into an altar. Surely they destroy the very power of life that throbs within the feast.

Christian pastors are shepherds of the flock of God, not priests in the temple of God.

5.   The Success of the Gospel (vs. 19)

In place of the law Christ has now brought in "a better hope, by which we draw near to God". The earlier priests were required to keep the people at a distance from God, behind the barriers of curtains, walls, and rituals; but our High Priest now carries us to the very throne of heaven! What does he mean, when he describes the gospel as a "better" hope?

(a) It is "better" because

- it has immeasurably superior qualities to the old law
- it brings with it greater advantage
- it is acceptable to all people and not one nation only
- it is entirely safe, being loved and received by children as well as their parents
- it has wider usefulness, richer promises, sweeter joys
- it is based on the more excellent principle of love in place of law
- it shows more skill in mending human ills, displays greater wisdom, ensures plainer virtue, promises lasting success.

Who then would wish to go back to the old way?

(b) It contains "hope" because, while its present blessings are numerous, it carries with it a desire of a yet greater good still to come. The gospel imparts a deep confidence about the future. Those who believe live with a well-founded expectation of an indescribable coming happiness.

(c) It is a "better hope" because it promises a better health, better happiness, better home, better honour.

AN IMPECCABLE PRIESTHOOD

- see Hebrews 7:20-28

We are now presented with the seven-fold glory of the priesthood of Christ -

A. HIS PRIESTHOOD IS ESTABLISHED BY OATH (vs. 20-21)

The old priesthood rested upon a law that was itself susceptible to change. From century to century its force fluctuated. It dealt with generations of people, with a nation, more than with persons. But this new priesthood is established in one Man by the sworn oath of God. Those former priests received their office from the hands of other men, within the legislature of their nation. Heaven was not always willing to confirm their priesthood. There were such men as Caiaphas, who was put in office by the Roman Emperor. But our Priest received his office direct from the hand of the King of Heaven. Notice the power of the declaration-

1. The Lord "said to Christ"

The expression loses its force in translation. "Said" in the original is a formal word. It means that God specifically designated Christ, and only Christ, to the office of High Priest. Before the assembled angels of heaven the Father formally addressed his Son and, saluting him, invested him with this glorious ministry of reconciliation and access.

2. This was done "with an oath"

Literally, an "asseveration on oath". It means "a strong assertion, a solemn affirmation, and a positive declaration" of the High Priesthood of Christ. The apostle could hardly have expressed himself more strongly. He declares in the most unequivocal terms the absolute certainty of the priestly office of Christ. This use of an oath by God is arresting. When men and women make a statement on oath, they call God to endorse the truth of what they say. They need to do this because their bare word is not reckoned sufficient. But could you say that about God? Surely his simple word is always entirely reliable? What would move the Lord to add to his promise a sworn oath? We see here a matter of such extraordinary importance that God was willing to go to extreme lengths to compel our earnest attention. What was that matter? We are speaking of nothing less than the infinite value of the High Priestly ministry of Christ.

3. *"The Lord has sworn ... "*

The writer is quoting the prophecy of Psalm 110:4. Though originally penned by the psalmist, the oracle-speaker was actually God. With an unalterable vow, the Father solemnly declared that nothing could prevent the fulfilment of his promise. He inflexibly bound himself to its complete performance. Then, to make it inconceivable that the promise should fail, he adds -

4. *"And will never change his mind"*

Having made this decision, having resolved to follow this course, nothing can persuade God to regret his promise, nor will he ever change his mind concerning it. So, with a glad heart, we may look to Jesus. With deep joy we may repeat the Father's words to the Son: "You are a Priest for ever!"

B. HIS PRIESTHOOD IS PERSONALLY GUARANTEED (vs. 22)

"By such measure" - that is, by the strength, power, and immense force of God's solemn oath - Jesus has become the "Guarantor" of a better covenant.

1. *What is meant by "Guarantor"?*

(a) Here is another word that in the NT occurs only in Hebrews. It is a legal word, and means that Jesus has pledged himself to perform everything required of a priest. Stronger still, it means that Jesus has become a "bondsman" to this ministry - he has willingly enslaved himself to it. Priesthood is now his urgent task. Why did he do this? For this reason: he longed to see his people enjoying freedom from anxiety and living in perfect security.

(b) The word also carries the sense of ratification - as if the sworn oath were still not enough. Therefore Jesus adds to the promise of an eternal priesthood the guarantee of his own person.

One could perhaps remain unimpressed by an impersonal promise. But in the person of Jesus we have living evidence of its truth. He makes it sure; in him we have a stable foundation; in him we find the grounds of our hope of eternal security.

(c) The word also means to "go bail". That is, Jesus has pledged himself to pay the price for our failure. He guarantees an adequate compensation for the loss and damage caused by sin. Every trace of our iniquity will be removed, and the demands of God's justice fully satisfied. Praise God!

2. He was made the surety of a better "covenant", a word that in Greek carries a triple significance -

(a) Disposition

In this new covenant the Lord has devised a better means of distributing his benefits to his people. Now the superabundant blessings of God flow out to all nations, not just to the Jews. By this the Father shows that his prevailing motive is love not law. He yearns to draw all people to the altar of mercy, not the bar of judgment. He is inclined more to kindness than to kindled wrath.

(b) Contract

When he established the eternal High Priesthood of Christ, the Lord made an agreement, in which he binds himself (on condition of trust in Christ) to show mercy and to forbear judgment. But this agreement requires a mutual promise: on our part, to love God with all our heart; on God's part, to open the way into his bountiful presence. This is a contract based on heavenly law and the integrity of God. It has as its cause the perfect obedience and suffering of the Son of God. The writing that contains this contract stands open before angels and mankind. It is sealed with the Blood of the Redeemer, which obligates God to fulfil all its terms. What is this writing? It is none other than "The New Testament of our Lord and Saviour Jesus Christ."

(c) Devisory

This term refers to a legal will in which gifts are freely bequeathed to the beneficiaries. We are those who benefit by heaven's "devisory will". And what are those benefits? Who could ever name them! Two passages may encompass them in a measure -

> "How shall we respond to these things? If God is for us, who can be against us? Since he did not spare his own Son, but delivered him to death for us all, surely he will now with Christ freely give us everything he has promised!" (Ro 8:31-32)

"This is what is written: no eye has ever seen, nor any ear heard, neither has anyone ever grasped the things God has prepared for those who love him. But God has now shown them to us by his Spirit!" (1 Co 2:9-10)

C. HIS PRIESTHOOD IS UNCHANGEABLE

"How many of those former priests there had to be, because death stopped them from remaining in office!" (vs. 23)

Some were good priests, and the people wept when they passed away. Others were evil. They turned many aside, and brought a curse upon God. Those who were faithful died with sorrow, knowing that their work remained unfinished. The people, bereft of their solace, remained scattered and lost. Yet so it must be for any earthly priesthood. Then out of the darkness shone the light of Christ. Unsurpassable in greatness, he has established a priesthood that is

1. Imperishable

"Because he lives for ever, Jesus has an endless priesthood that cannot be passed onto another" (vs. 24)

Once again the apostle employs a word from law and commerce: "non-transmissible". It could describe a man who had bound himself to remain in a certain place. He would stay at his task either until it was completed or his services were no longer required. He would not delegate the burden to another, but undertook to fulfil it himself. The word could also describe a person who was party to a legal contract, and had therefore sworn to honour his liabilities. It could refer to the obligation of a slave to render full service to his master, or to a soldier's duty to remain at his post until relieved by his commanding officer.

For us it means that Jesus will never turn away from the Cross. Nor will he ever cast off his priestly robe. He will never weary of his office, nor fail to honour his promise, nor prove unworthy of our trust.

Could this be possible? Does God love us so much that he is willing to apply worldly terms like these to himself? It seems scarcely credible; yet it must be true, for he attests it by a sworn oath! How marvellous then is his love! How unending must be our praise!

2. *Immutable*

Can anything more be added to what he has already revealed? Surely the cup of blessing is full and brimming over by now? But no, in a fury of inspiration the apostle rushes on. He adds more and more superlatives to this all-transcendent Priesthood. He says that "Jesus must remain for ever." The idea is that his life is indestructible, and therefore his ministry must be perpetual. The Priest is indestructible, therefore his office is immutable, and his strength invincible. Now how could terms such as these be used of any human priesthood? Such glory as this can belong only to the Son of God. See the strength of this Priesthood:

- no power in earth or heaven is able to wound it
- it can never be susceptible to change
- the promise it holds will shine bright for all eternity
- nothing can break or limit its provisions
- it will never be passed on to another
- forever it is invested in the Son of God
- no sin can pollute it
- all human transgression is lost in its greatness
- it will never be interrupted or hindered
- its efficacy is constant for everyone everywhere.

So there will never be a vacancy in the Priesthood of heaven. You cannot imagine a day nor an hour when we shall lack a priest to care for our interests and to stand for us before God.

CHAPTER EIGHT:

INTERCESSOR

Text: Hebrews 7:23-28.

INTRODUCTION

"One after the other, how many priests there have been! Death has prevented each one of them from continuing in office. But Jesus lives on for ever! Therefore he has an eternal priesthood; and because he is always there to plead their cause, he is able to save absolutely everyone who approaches God through him." (vs. 23-25).

"Christ is ABLE!" That single, incredible idea runs through all three verses of our text, which in Greek is just one tumultuous sentence, its words stumbling over themselves in excitement.

Yesterday, today, forever, "Christ is able!" In the face of every circumstance, in the presence of every need, "Christ is able!" Across the ages the great declaration stands firm and unchanged: "Christ is ABLE!" Confronting every threat of poverty, disease, sin, and even death, it remains serene and sure. It was there when you were weeping yesterday; it is there despite your trouble today; it will still be there when you need it tomorrow: "Christ is ABLE!"

You cannot conceive any situation, any hurt, any loss, any trauma that could suddenly make the apostle's affirmation untrue. No privation, no pain can sap its vitality. No defeat, no failure can exhaust its potential. Wherever you are, whatever you face, still it stands in scripture: "Christ is ABLE!" To every exigency in life, there is only one response the believing heart can make: "Christ is ABLE!"

Yet someone may still ask: "Just how great is his ability? In what direction does it lie? Where is it focussed? Is he more powerful to save in some ways than in others?"

At once we discover an ambiguity in the Greek: the adverb may refer either to degree or time, and it can join grammatically with either *"able"* or *"save"*. So it could be translated in any of these ways:

- "absolutely able to save" - no limit in <u>concept</u>: no human need lies outside its compass; no hurt can outreach its promise
- "forever able to save" - no limit in <u>existence</u>: for as long as Christ reigns in the heavenlies he will bear the name Saviour
- "able to save for ever" - no limit in <u>duration</u>: this is not a temporary nor a restricted salvation, but will span the endless ages
- "able to save absolutely" - no limit in <u>prowess</u>: Christ has strength to heal the most malignant disease, to free the most wretched victim, to bring heaven into the deepest hell, and to supplant the most tormented grief with joy!

Perhaps the apostle deliberately intended this ambiguity to show how infinite, without boundaries, is the power of Jesus to save.

This great salvation stems from the priestly ministry of Christ, which the apostle continues to contrast with the Aaronic priesthood -

THE PREVENTED PRIESTS

"There were many of those priests, since death <u>prevented</u> them from continuing in office" (vs. 23).

Let me briefly take up this theme again from our previous chapter. A passage from Josephus (20:10) dramatically illustrates the impermanence of the old priesthood –

> "And now I think it proper and agreeable to history to give an account of our high priests; how they began, who those are which are capable of that dignity, and how many of them there (have) been ... In the first place, therefore, history informs us that Aaron, the brother of Moses, officiated to God as a high priest; and that, after his death, his sons succeeded him immediately; and that this divinity hath been continued down from them all to their posterity. whence it is a custom of our country, that no one should take the high priesthood of God but he who is of the blood of Aaron, while every one that is of another stock, though he were a king, can never obtain the high priesthood.
>
> "Accordingly, the number of all the high priests from Aaron ... until Phanas ... was eighty-three; of whom

thirteen officiated as high priests (from the time of
Moses) until King Solomon erected the temple to God
Now these thirteen, who were the descendants of two of
the sons of Aaron, received this dignity by succession,
one after another ... (and) the number of years during the
rule of these thirteen ... was six hundred and twelve.

'After those thirteen high priests, eighteen took the high
priesthood at Jerusalem, one in succession to the other,
from the days of king Solomon until Nebuchadnezzar ...
; the time of these high priests were four hundred and
sixty six years, six months, and ten days

> - the list continues, until it reaches Jacimus,
c 170 B.C.

Now when Jacimus had retained the priesthood three
years, he died, and there was no one that succeeded him,
but the city continued seven years without a high priest.
(But then) they appointed Jonathan to be their high priest
(until he was murdered, and replaced by Simon, who
was also murdered, and replaced by Hyrcanus, who held
the office for thirty years) ... etc ...

thus, as Josephus said, and as scripture confirms, the sad procession
began with Aaron -

> *"Moses removed from Aaron the ceremonial robes, and
> gave them instead to his son Eleazar. Aaron died while
> they were still on the mountain top, and only then did
> Afoses and Eleazar came down. All the people saw that
> Aaron had died, and the entire community mourned for
> him for thirty days."*[22]

So Eleazar took his father Aaron's place. But of him too, as of all who
followed him, it was eventually said: *"and he died."* Which brings us to
consider -

THE PERMANENT PRIEST

'Because he lives for ever, he has a <u>Permanent</u> priesthood" (vs. 24).

---

[22] Numbers 20:28.

How much better than those priests is the priesthood of Jesus:

- they were many: he is one
- their term was short: he is a priest forever
- they were sinners: he is undefiled
- they offered animals: he offered himself
- death conquered them: he conquered death!

THE POWERFUL PRIEST

'He is able to save <u>completely</u> everyone who comes to God through him"

We ask again: how powerful is this great salvation? Its strength is proportionate to the peril we were in! Notice the phrase *"come to God"*. It shows that the crisis we faced was one of *separation:*

- from God: for ever
- from each other: in lonely isolation
- from ourselves: in the broken disorder of sin
- from the kingdom: and our appointed destiny

Christ came to end that disjunction, to tear down the barriers, to create on earth a foretaste of the endless joy of fellowship that is the hallmark of heaven.

Further, he says that Christ saves us *"completely"*; or literally, *"to-the-fulness"*. The Greek word occurs only in one other place, *Luke 13:11,* where it describes a crippled woman whom Jesus healed. After he had spoken to her, she stood up straight, reaching now to her full height. What a picture we see of the state of humanity - crippled, bowed down, oppressed by Satan. But the touch of the Master's hand can make us tall again, loosed from our fetters, restored to the liberty of the children of God.

Some think our text in *Hebrews* should be translated *"to the Completion"*. If so, then it means we shall be so well saved that nothing can prevent us from reaching our appointed destiny in the coming Kingdom Age. What God has begun he will finish! We will surely see the "completion" of the Father's plan. How gladly we may affirm our confidence: "The Lord will keep me until that Day; I trust him to bring me to my inheritance!"

So we cry that Jesus is able to save! Without qualification, without limitation! There is no sinner so great, no iniquity so scarlet that Jesus cannot remove it. No sinner falls into irrecoverable ruin until he dies in his sin. While he has breath in his body, Jesus is able to save him - to abolish the penalty of his past sin, to break the power of present sin.

This *"uttermost"* salvation is salvation in the highest degree, the greatest salvation heaven can provide. We who believe know that Christ has saved us completely, perfectly, fully, for ever. We know that the Lord has done the most that can be done to lift us from sin to the utmost height of happiness.

Further, this salvation belongs freely to all those who come to God in the name of Jesus. How is this so? Because Jesus is ever

THE PRAYING PRIEST

"He always lives to intercede for us!" (vs. 25)

We ask: how does this Priest achieve this magnificent salvation? We might expect another answer, for the one given is surely surprising: 'he intercedes!

Think what he might have said:

- Jesus saves to the uttermost by unleashing his majestic omnipotence
- Jesus saves to the uttermost by destroying sin with a fiery blast
- Jesus saves to the uttermost by sending many angels to rescue his people
- Jesus saves to the uttermost by expending all the treasures of heaven
- and the like, all of them dramatic, energetic, powerful ways to salvation.

Yet the apostle ignores those obvious responses to the question. Instead he offers a solution that seems by comparison colourless and unexciting. He simply says: Jesus *"makes intercession"* for us!

Who in a thousand years would have guessed such a response? It is such an unexpected and improbable saying, that it has the ring of truth! It is, as they say, not *what* you know, but *who!*

But what is this intercession?

It is certainly not like that of Aristippus, a Greek philosopher who flourished around 400 B.C. He came to the tyrant Dionysius to beg a favour for a friend; the tyrant refused. Aristippus continued pleading and finally prostrated himself before Dionysius. Seeing him lying there, kissing his feet, Dionysius finally granted Aristippus his request. Later, when his friends castigated him for low behaviour unworthy of a philosopher, Aristippus retorted: "But that is where the tyrant's ears are!"

Our Advocate does not stand with tears, hands outstretched, desperately pleading. Even less need he abase himself before the divine throne. You will not find him begging a reluctant Deity to show mercy. Rather he asks as a Prince seated at the Father's right hand! You should see him there by faith: ever in the presence of God, always active, always serving, always officiating as Priest. Within the veil, in the Holy Place, the Saviour never stops petitioning God to bestow grace upon us. He is there now, acting to remove the variance that cut us asunder from each other and from God, making reconciliation, uniting us in love.

Listen! At this moment, while you trustfully breathe his name, by faith you can hear him soliciting the favour of God for you. Will he be heard? How can you doubt it, for is he not the Son, greatly loved by the Father? Whatever he asks will be granted!

THE PRISTINE PRIEST

"This is just the kind of High Priest we needed: one who is holy, free of sin, gentle, standing apart from sinners, and exalted above the' heavens" (vs. 26).

At last we reach the purpose that from the beginning of his letter has pulled the writer onwards. So far he has demonstrated the futility of the levitical system, whose priests were not suited to the real needs of fallen humanity. But in Jesus we have a High Priest who is perfectly adapted to all our hurts; he fulfils every necessity of God and the people. See the brilliant character of Christ, expressed in the words of the old version -

(A) "HOLY"

Jesus was utterly faithful in his performance of every task required of him by his Father. Nor will you find in him any habit of sin, nor even so much as the least inclination to sin. Though evil lurks in the lives of even the most saintly of Christians, not the slightest shadow of transgression darkened the heart of Christ. He was man, but he was a man without sin.

And still he is holy, still he is faithful, still he carries out meticulously his Father's will.

(B) "HARMLESS"

What causes harm? Sin! But Jesus having no sin is unable to harm - that is, to harm outside the processes of law. As Judge and Executor of the law of God, he will one day pass sentence on those who refuse to embrace his salvation; but to his people he is harmless. They have no fear of him; they only delight in his presence. Those who love him trust him wholly, for they know he cannot deceive, nor do them any violence.

(C) "UNDEFILED"

How different is this testimony from that of the old priesthood. There a sinful man first had to present an atonement for his own sin; only then was he free to offer a sacrifice for the nation. But here we have a Priest who is free from stain; he is therefore able to present a perfect sacrifice for the whole world. Further, Christ is not only free from personal blemish, but also from the defilement of other men's sins. How unlike us he is! Though we may be sometimes free of deliberate transgression yet we stay defiled by the sins of our forefathers and the sins of our contemporaries. How often we contribute to the faults of other people by wrong example, careless actions, faulty behaviour! We are altogether defiled: our High Priest is altogether undefiled. Let our hearts bow before him in grateful praise.

(D) "SEPARATE"

He was a man, yet was separated from the sin in man by his unique birth. While we incur guilt from our natural and inescapable union with Adam (our father), Christ had God as his Father, and was born free of sin. In this he is different from us sinners, a perfect Man, able to understand people, yet separated from them. However, he is not separated from us in aloof disdain. Rather, he stands apart from us only in our sin and so that he might bring us into unity with God. For this cause his entrance into the holiest in heaven has again separated him from sinners. Nothing defiled can ever enter those sacred precincts, at the throne of God. But Christ has gone before us to prepare the way, and he is working now to fit us to follow in his steps.

(E) "HIGHER"

Christ, says the apostle, now stands *"higher than the heavens"*. In the former phrase *("separate from sinners"),* we learned about Christ's perfection as Son of Man. Now we view his perfection as Son of God. The one expresses his humanity, the other his deity. His ascension exalted him higher than all the heavens, and set him at the right hand of the Majesty on High. There his intercessory ministry continues across the ages; there he purposes to bring his people. The phrase may also refer (as do the four previous expressions) to Christ's personal holiness. *"Higher than the heavens"* -that is, in holiness he stands purer than heaven itself, more chaste than the virtuous angels. For they, while they may be holy, are yet able to fall into sin (as did many in their ancient rebellion), and are prevented from doing so only by the election of God. But Christ is more than simply "innocent" - he is the very essence of holiness. Therefore he is able to impart probity to all who come to God by him. Who else can do this? It lies beyond the power of even the noblest angel. So Christ is *"made higher than the heavens*

What a wonderful heritage is ours who expect to be brought with Christ to this glory *'within ... (and) beyond the veil"*. Now we know why the saints are destined to judge the angels and to rule the heavens! Let us labour diligently to secure this magnificent prize!

THE PERFECTED PRIEST

The apostle now completes his proof of the establishment of a new and more glorious priesthood in Christ. He also introduces his next theme: the perfect sacrifice of Christ, which is the seal of God's New and Better Covenant. See it then in verses 27 and 28, which are here given in a free rendering -

> *"Each of the priests of the old order were bound by necessity to offer sacrifices day by day - firstly for their own sins, and then for the sins of the people. This was the great stumbling block that caused the failure of the old covenant. But Christ has no such daily necessity. Being himself perfect and free from sin, he met every requirement of God's law when he brought himself to the altar of sacrifice and offered himself once to God. The law appointed ordinary men to be high priest. Since they*

were frail, weak, sinful, dying human beings, they failed. That is why the Spirit of God spoke through the psalmist long after the law had been established and promised that a new priesthood would come. He did not speak about many priests and many sacrifices. Instead, by a strong oath God chose one Priest: namely his Son. This appointment is complete and permanent. It will never be abrogated. So we have as our High Priest the Son of God, made perfect for ever, and consecrated eternally to his ministry of mercy and reconciliation."

CHAPTER NINE:

MEDIATOR

No one knows who wrote the letter to the Hebrews. Several centuries passed by before Paul's name became commonly attached to it. However we do know that the author was a cultured and literate person, who wrote a splendidly cadenced Greek - at times lyrical, and always perfectly structured. He (or perhaps she) was deeply immersed in the gospel, and utterly captivated by a vision of Jesus, whom he portrays in seven magnificent tableaus (1:3 to 7:28) -

> Jesus - the express image of God
> Jesus - superior to Angels
> Jesus - superior to Death
> Jesus - superior to Moses
> Jesus - superior to Joshua
> Jesus - superior to Aaron
> Jesus - superior to Abraham.

Those tableaus occupy the first two major sections of the letter. Now we come to the third major section (8:1 to 10:18). Here the apostle reaches a peak in his argument, beginning with the words: "Here is the main point of everything I have written so far." He means both that he plans to summarise his previous chapters, and that his argument has now reached its goal. The time has come for him to state the real burden of his heart. All that he wrote before was only the foundation for what he is eager to write now.

The summary is this. He has outlined the surpassing glory of the priesthood of Melchizedek. Then he says plainly, "We have such a High Priest," one who provides perfect satisfaction to both the justice of God and the cry of the human heart. Mark the words: "We have him"! Christ is already ours. The wonder of that saying cannot be fully grasped, not even by the wisest of the redeemed. We can do no more than bow in grateful acquiescence before such incomprehensible grace. What remains except to receive the goodness of the Lord?

If we are possessors of Christ, do we then become masters of the Lord of Glory? No, for scripture says that we have a beneficiary relationship with him. He gives; we receive. True, he has obligated himself to offer us love, consideration, protection, help, provision, which does give us a claim on Christ. But we may exercise that right only so long as we return to him what is his right: our fullest respect, worship, obedience, and (chiefest of all) trust.

The declaration is positive, emphatic, a present reality: "We have such a High Priest!" What kind of priest? A royal priest, after the order of Melchizedek - a High Priest who has devoted himself to our service, who is ordained to act for us.

Have you sinned? Then fly to Jesus for refuge and beg him to present to the Father the atonement that belongs to you. Do you desire access to the presence of God? Then trust your High Priest to open a way for you through the veil. Do you need someone to intercede for you? Then you may confidently commit your case to your Priest, who will never fail in his intercession. Since you have a Priest, a High Priest, such a High Priest, do not be laggard in availing yourself of his willing service. That is how you can do him the highest honour and bring to yourself his untold blessing.

That brings us to our text for this chapter: Hebrews 8:1-6

Christ is a Priest unlike any other the world has ever seen. Every other priesthood was but a shadow of his; in him the divine pattern of priesthood has been eternally established. Here is how the writer of Hebrews describes it -

THE MAJESTY OF THE PRIEST

> *"Everything I have said so far comes to this: we have such a High Priest, who now sits at the right hand of the throne of the Majesty in the heavens" (8:1).*

By an immutable decree, God appointed Christ High Priest forever. No other can usurp his position, nor ever take his place. Our High Priest is seated where no one but he can ever sit: beside the Majesty on high. He is there as an equal, at the side of God, ever able to make strong intercession in response to the cry of his people. Notice the following -

A. "AT THE RIGHT HAND"

The phrase "at the right hand" speaks of his exaltation to the place of highest honour. It shows his strength, his activity, and his diligence. The richness of what it means appears in the following -

> *"Your right hand, O Lord, possesses majestic power; your right hand, O Lord, smashes your enemies to pieces! In your exalted greatness you threw down everyone who rose up against you. You blazed with fury; you consumed them like stubble" (Ex 15:6-7).*

Our High Priest is that Right Hand of God, immense in power, and splendid in glory. He has strength to save, and ability to judge. It is his right to execute the wrath of God, to condemn the enemies of God. His greatness and his excellency are far beyond telling.

> *"The Lord came from Sinai, and his glory shone down from Seir; from Mount Paran his splendour spread over them. He came with thousands of his holy ones, while fiery judgment streamed out from his right hand. Yet his own people he loves, and for them his hand carries only blessing. Therefore they sit humbly in his presence waiting for his instruction" (De 33:2-3)*

The Right Hand of the Majesty on High, who is Christ our Priest, has become Captain of the thousands of his saints. The laws of heaven are established and administered by him. Yet because he is so mighty in power, he is also able to be merciful in love. Therefore his hand carries two things: wrath for the ungodly; safety for the godly.

> *"You will show me the path of life; your presence brings me infinite joy; at your right hand my happiness will never end" (Ps 16:11)*

Why is Christ sitting at God's right hand? So that he can bring us to the same place. Indeed, to reach the throne of God we need only keep pressing toward Christ, for where he is there is the throne. Nor need we wait until we pass the veil of death, for the line may also be translated: "at your right hand there are now pleasures that shall continue for evermore." The key lies in following the psalmist's example: "I keep my eye always on the Lord; while he is beside me, nothing can shake me!" (vs 8).

Those who turn to God will find God turning to them. Upon them the blessing of God's Right Hand will fall: the Lord will be their "portion" and their "inheritance"; their pathway will travel through "pleasant places"; they will receive a "bountiful reward" (vs. 5-7). How glad we should be who know the Right Hand of God!

In many other scriptures that mention "the right hand of God" we may see a picture of Christ -

> *"Let me see more of your marvellous love, O Lord! Are you not the One who saves by your right hand everyone who fully trusts you?" (Ps 17:7).*

> *"Only your right hand keeps me standing tall; I am honoured by the way you have stooped down to lift me up" (Ps 18:35).*

> *"I know that the Lord will always rescue his chosen one; from heaven God will answer prayer with all the victorious power of his right hand" (Ps 20:6).*

> *"How can the one you love be rescued unless you hear from heaven and save with your right hand?" (Ps 60:5).*

> *"Let your hand be upon the Man of your Right Hand, upon the Son of Man whom you made strong for yourself!" (Ps 80:17).*

> *"Sing a new anthem to the Lord, for he has done marvellous things; by his right hand and his holy arm he has triumphed over every enemy" (Ps 98:1).*

> *"Sounds of laughter and shouts of victory come from the tents of the righteous, for the right hand of the Lord has behaved **valiantly**. The right hand of the Lord is exalted! The right hand of the Lord has behaved valiantly!" (Ps 118:15-16).*

We who know Christ see in all those places a description of the matchless splendour, the mighty strength, the limitless ability of our glorious High Priest.

B. "OF THE THRONE"

He who was born in humility now reigns in splendour. This marks him truly as a Priest who is of the order of Melchizedek - a Royal Priest, both Monarch and Mediator. Christ sits beside the central throne of the universe, possessing all power and authority; therefore he merits all respect and reverence. He is clothed with unequalled grandeur and splendid dignity; he is sole disposer of heaven's wealth, the zenith of heaven's majesty.

C. "OF THE MAJESTY"

That phrase depicts the central point of heaven's glory, the lofty pinnacle where the dazzling lustre of heaven is concentrated. There our Royal Priest reigns as unquestioned Prince, supreme sovereign of the entire universe.

D. "IN THE HEAVENS"

In this context the word "heavens" describes the original, primeval part of God's creation: "In the beginning God created the heavens and (then) the earth." The "heavens" occupy that part of space where the Lord God, the omnipresent Deity, has localised his infinite glory and has made his presence manifest. There the angels have permission to gather in the audience of God; there the saints will obtain their eternal reward.

HE MINISTRY OF THE PRIEST

"Our High Priest is a minister of the true tabernacle, and of the sanctuary pitched, not on earth by a man, but in heaven by God" (He 8:2)

A. OUR HIGH PRIEST IS A MINISTER

The word "minister" is an arresting one. It means "public servant", "benefactor", "functionary". It shows that Christ has placed himself at the service of mankind, denying his own interests, surrendering his own rights. He has done this entirely at his own expense, with a view solely to providing the benefits of salvation to all who believe. This is his sacred office, this is the trust he has received from his Father. He will never violate it.

B. HE IS A MINISTER OF THE TRUE TABERNACLE

The simple meaning of "tabernacle" is "tent", which suggests there is a place in heaven where the Lord God dwells. Not that he stands in need of any dwelling; but he graciously makes it possible for angels and his people to find him there.

He calls it the "true" tabernacle because the one Moses erected in the wilderness was at best an imperfect copy of the heavenly original. The desert tabernacle was put together by skilled artisans; but the divine tabernacle was pitched in heaven by the hand of God. That true sanctuary is therefore greater by far than the ancient copy, and, unlike Israel's tent, will never be moved. Even so, it is still called a "tent". Why? Perhaps because one day, when all the sons of God have been brought to perfection, it too will have no further value. When righteousness holds supreme sway perhaps the heavenly tabernacle too will be discarded. But, while it stands, this tabernacle is true: it is real, it is the original, it supplants all others. There is nothing false, nothing doubtful, nothing deceptive in this tabernacle: it will accomplish its designed purpose. Even now we can enter it, and live under its protecting roof.

If human hands make a tabernacle, a tent, a church, then human hands can destroy it. But this tabernacle is pitched by God, and no one can move it. Therefore its priesthood also is fixed, and cannot shift to another place. That is why Christ ministers there, at the heavenly tabernacle, and there alone. Learn this: those who rely upon any sanctuary made with human hands will find disappointment and preclude themselves from the priestly ministry of Christ. A church building is not the tabernacle of the Lord - it has value only as a temporal gathering place for saints, whose real hope is fixed in the heavenly sanctuary.

C. HE IS A MINISTER OF THE SANCTUARY

"Sanctuary" means the innermost part of the Tabernacle, the "Holy of Holies":

- if he ministers there, then he too must be perfect in holiness;
- if he will one day bring us there, then we too must be transformed by him into that same marvellous perfection.

It is called a "sanctuary" because there the hunted find refuge, the weak receive strong protection, and the storm-tossed anchor in a safe haven. And the wonder is that, by faith, we may even now enter this sanctuary and share its rich blessing, its quiet fellowship, its unassailable security.

THE MISSION OF THE PRIEST

"Every high priest is ordained for a purpose: to offer gifts and sacrifices. Therefore this man must also have something to offer. Yet if he were on earth he could not even be a priest, for a legally established and exclusive priesthood already exists" (8:3-4).

In the old order, each high priest offered the gifts and sacrifices brought to him by the people. That was the essential function of priesthood. But how can a Priest in heaven, ministering unseen in an unseen sanctuary, fulfil this duty? He cannot handle human gifts or sacrifices. Yet he must have something to offer, else he is not a Priest. What does he then offer? The apostle does not answer that question here - in fact he does not answer it until the twelfth verse of the next chapter. He merely agrees "that this Man must have something to offer". However that poses a problem. If he does not offer the legally appointed sacrifices, surely his ministry is invalid? Not so, says the apostle, and then shows how scripture itself prevents him from offering the gifts and sacrifices that were formerly presented -

First, he states the obvious: even if Christ were on earth he could not be a priest. The only legitimate earthly priesthood was that which sprang from Levi - but Jesus came from the line of Judah (7:14). Though he was the Son of God he could not lawfully serve at the altar in Jerusalem. So then, if he is to be Priest, he must be Priest in heaven, outside the old law. That means he must also offer a new gift, a new sacrifice, one that suits the heavenly sanctuary.

Second: he states that the earthly tabernacle was a copy of the heavenly tabernacle, and therefore inferior to it. This he proves from scripture, which tells about the original divine pattern of the tabernacle -

THE MODEL OF THE PRIEST

"The temple in which the levitical priests minister is a symbolic copy of the heavenly sanctuary. That is why,

> *when Moses was about to build his tabernacle in the*
> *desert, God told him, `Make sure to follow exactly the*
> *pattern I showed you on the mountain" (8:5).*

The earthly tabernacle was a copy, a foreshadowing, of the eternal, divine ideal. Does this leave us free to despise it? No, for it did follow the pattern of the heavenly, and therefore held greater glory than any other building ever erected on earth. Yet it became a bane instead of a blessing. The people forgot that it was only a copy; they began to treat it as though it were the first and greatest of sanctuaries. It began to obscure instead of reveal the heavenly sanctuary. A mere shadow replaced the divine reality.

Yet God's instructions were clear enough, and recorded in scripture: "Make sure to follow exactly the pattern I showed you on the mountain." Moses apparently saw in a vision the original blueprint, or the true model, of God's sanctuary. Then with remarkable skill he and his helpers translated it into earthly form. The pattern they followed was ancient - prepared from the beginning of human history - for its sacrificial Lamb was slain from the foundation of the world. The anonymous author of The Wisdom of Solomon refers to this -

> "You commanded them to build a sanctuary on your
> holy mountain, and an altar in the city where you dwell;
> it was a copy of the heavenly tabernacle that *you*
> *prepared long ago, in the very beginning"* (9:8).

There is a picture here of us, for we too reflect a heavenly pattern. We are made "in the image of God." Therefore learn that you will find reality, not on earth, but in heaven. This world is but a shadow cast by the heavenly glory.

The expression "shadow" was familiar to Greek people in those days. It was a common term in philosophy, where the Greeks used it to convey the idea that everything on earth has a better, more glorious counterpart in heaven. Plato expressed this idea in his famous parable. He likened the human race to a group of prisoners who were chained in a deep cave, with their faces to the back wall, and prevented by their fetters from turning around. Outside the cave, people constantly moved to and fro, casting flickering shadows on the prisoners' wall. That was all they could see of the outside world, that was all they knew of its inhabitants. Eventually some of the prisoners decided that there was no better, brighter world, that the shadows were only hallucination. Also, they had become so accustomed to darkness, their eyes would have been blinded if they had faced the light.

That is how many people still are. The shadowy glimmers of this world have bemused them into supposing that their dark cave is the only reality. They have forgotten the immensely greater and brighter dimension that lies beyond this earthly sphere. May God help us never to become so dazed by the things we see around us that we deny the reality of the heavenly world. Perhaps we cannot yet see it clearly, but those who look will see many reflections from that world cast across their path.

Note also that the pattern was shown to Moses "on the mountain" - when he was alone with God. The Lord has a plan for your life. Climb the mountain of prayer and consecration and God will surely make himself known to you.

THE MEDIATION OF THE PRIEST

> *"Jesus is the mediator of a better covenant established upon better promises; therefore God has given him a ministry far superior to the old priesthood" (8:6)*

The apostle has already shown that Jesus has a ministry that is "far superior" to that of the levitical priesthood. Their ministry was of the order of Aaron; his is of the order of Melchizedek, a ministry that is more excellent because of its greater eminence, its better qualities. But he has already told us all this. Why does he repeat it? Because an idea has struck him. We know that God has given Jesus the highest office. Yet this cannot have any value for us if his ministry must still be channelled through the old covenant, the old sacrifices, the old promises. He can have a better ministry only if it is greater than the old covenant by so much as the new priesthood is greater than the old priesthood.

Three wonderful things are stated...

A. CHRIST IS THE MEDIATOR

How much we stand in need of a mediator. Job cried out -

> *"God is not a man, as I am; so how can I argue with him, how can I haul him into court and charge him with fraud? If only I could find someone to act as arbitrator,*

someone able to compel both of us to accept his impartial decision!" (Jb 9:32-33).

Job wanted an *"arbitrator"* - someone who could adjudicate between himself and God, who would plead his cause. This is what Jesus has become for us - a mediator. That is, *"one who stands in the middle between two people and brings them together."* He was also someone who stood surety, or went bail, for another, who guaranteed to pay a debt. When people stand at variance with God, they should cry to Jesus for assistance. He, our Great High Priest, will act immediately to remove the difference, to break down the barrier, to effect full reconciliation. Especially, Christ is the Mediator of the new covenant. He draws both God and the believer to that covenant and binds them to it, thus making it the common ground upon which both heaven and earth meet.

B. CHRIST IS THE MEDIATOR OF A BETTER COVENANT

He has entered into a binding contract to provide all those things the old covenant failed to provide. This is a superior agreement, a more noble testament. It brings greater happiness and greater honour. It is "better" because it deals with heaven as well as earth, reality in place of shadow, soul as well as body, eternity as well as time.

C. THIS COVENANT IS ESTABLISHED UPON BETTER PROMISES

Those who claim the "better" promise of this new covenant will find it steadfast and sure. To them it will give stability and peace, and an unassailable hope. It is established on the firm and permanent basis of God's unchanging love; it is settled unalterably in his "mercy that endures for ever". Ratified by the oath of God, sealed by the pierced hand of Christ, it is able to take hold of the trembling heart and make it strong against every fiery dart flung by the enemy.

Those who take hold of this covenant and its better promise will be brought into the secure sanctuary of God. There the Lord will be favourably inclined to them; there they will be kept safe from all lasting harm. His promise is sure: those who trust him will never suffer final loss nor defeat.

The living God has accepted this new covenant as the only legal and valid basis upon which men and women may approach him. But he has accepted it, has established it, and has made its better promise available to all who believe. Claim it then, with all boldness!

So we have looked at the heavenly sanctuary, and at the Priest of the sanctuary, and we have read an introduction to the covenant of which this Priest is the mediator. We are now to consider this better covenant in greater detail.

CHAPTER TEN:

COVENANTOR

Text: Hebrews 8:7-13

It was very bold of the apostle to write to Jews and to speak of a "new" and "better" covenant. Why? Because for centuries the Hebrew people had insisted that the covenant God made with Moses was the only divinely confirmed agreement on earth. However, before his readers could protest, the apostle reminded them that their own scriptures had foretold the coming of a new covenant. But why would God promise a new covenant if the first one had been perfect? The conclusion is inescapable: the old covenant must be replaced because it had many defects. There would have been no room for a new agreement if the first had not been faulty. He infers then:

- **first:** that the new covenant is "faultless"; it leads men and women to uprightness, and makes them innocent; it has no defect itself; no one will ever be able to charge it with failure, or censure it in any way; and
- **second:** that the old covenant has been "found faulty"; for those who examine it closely will see in it blemishes and imperfections: it was incomplete in itself, and could never bring more than an incomplete blessing.

Clearly the Lord himself found fault with the former covenant, for he said -

> *"The time is surely coming when I will make a new covenant with the house of Israel and the house of Judah" (vs. 8)*

Notice how he refuses to restrict the covenant to the Jews, but insists upon including the "House of Israel". His intention was to broaden the covenant to include all who may rightly claim membership in the covenant nation, whether by natural or spiritual descent.

This new covenant is founded in Jesus of Nazareth, a son of Israel, and it guarantees the final redemption and perpetuity of Israel as a nation (which Jeremiah predicted, Je 31:31-40). But while the new covenant (like the old one) does belong particularly to Israel, it also embraces every willing heart (see vs. 11).

Let us then consider the terms of the old covenant, and the terms of the new covenant -

THE TERMS OF THE OLD COVENANT

"My new covenant (says God) will not be like the one I made long ago with their ancestors when I brought them safely out of Egypt. They violated the terms of our agreement, so I stopped taking any notice of them" (8:9)

By contrast with the new covenant, notice that the old one was

- a covenant made with one nation through its "ancestors"
- a covenant based on the deliverance of Israel from Egypt
- a covenant conditional upon Israel's entry into Canaan
- a covenant of which Moses was mediator
- a covenant made with a reluctant people, based upon compulsion and fear
- a covenant so conditional upon human obedience that when its terms were broken, God could set it aside.

So the Lord withdrew his favour from Israel, and disregarded them.

THE TERMS OF THE NEW COVENANT

How unlike the former covenant is this new one! The Lord said: "This is the covenant that I will make with the people of Israel" -

A. FOUR DIVINE PROMISES *(He 9:10)*

1. *"I will put my laws into their minds, and inscribe them on their hearts"*

Here is no external law written on stone tablets, powerless to equip people to obey its precepts. Now they will heed God, not because of terror of punishment, but because of trust in his promise. Love, not legalism, is the prevailing principle of the new covenant. The Father will no longer have to lead an unwilling people into an unwanted land, for now his children gladly follow Christ into the longed-for heavenly home.

There was no moral lack in the old covenant; its fault lay in its inability to help even those people who wanted to observe its rules. Even less could it give anyone a disposition to obey. At best its precepts could be memorised, and some level of outward conformity to them achieved.

This new covenant, however, will not be something to be learned mechanically and coldly obeyed. People will understand it, they will remember it, it will satisfy the searchings of their intelligence. The Holy Spirit will burn it upon their innermost soul, so that it will become part of their being, the spring of life within them. The Lord will give them a strong will, a settled determination, to abide by its provisions. They will heed it willingly, gladly, constantly. They will know his law, believe it, observe it, judge it to be good, perform it in every way.

By writing this new covenant on the hearts of his servants, the Lord will create within them an affection for heavenly things, a passion for righteousness, a love of godliness, a grief for sin, and a courage to withstand every opposition. They will find only pleasure in their service for God, and will gladly walk in his way.

2. *"I will at last be their God, and they will finally be my people"*

How much is compassed in that one saying - "I will be their God!" The Lord will be to them riches, prosperity, help, comfort, guidance, strength, righteousness, peace, mercy, healing, provision - and ten thousand more blessings! He will be everything they could ever require - they will never lack any good thing: they will never be enslaved by any evil thing.

If the Lord is their God, then he will say, "They will be my people." As his people, they are his subjects and must keep his laws. But the difference and glory of this new covenant is that God enables his people to do his will. He puts within them all they need to please him; he plants in their lives the fruitful trees of love, faith, hope and righteousness.

Notice the word "covenant", which normally describes an agreement between two persons who undertake to do certain things for their mutual benefit. If either party breaks the conditions laid down, the covenant is void. That is what happened under the old covenant. But the Greek word the apostle uses here would be better translated "testament" or "will". Now a will cannot be altered by a second party. Once it is written and the death of the testator takes place, the will remains fixed for ever. It may be rejected by the beneficiaries, but it cannot be changed unless its provisions are illegal. That does sometime happen in human courts; but at the heavenly bar no one will ever successfully plead for the annulment of the "New Testament" of our great High Priest. His death brought into force a will that is faultless.

So God has made his covenant, described under the terminology of a will. We may either receive it or reject it. But whatever we do, God has still set his terms, laid down his purpose, and established his will. Nobody can bargain with the Lord; he will make no other covenant. The death of Jesus has fixed the heavenly testament irrevocably and for ever.

3.   *"Everyone will know me, from the least to the greatest" (vs. 11)*

In Israel, the common people often lived in spiritual darkness, while religion was a privilege of the upper classes. No-one bothered to teach ordinary men and women the way of God. Despised, often too poor to bring an animal for sacrifice, the lower classes were oppressed by extortionate priests and crushed by a maze of regulations that working people could not hope to observe.

Jesus exposed that scandalous state when he purged the Temple (Jn 2:13-16; Mt 21:12-14). He angrily denounced the scribes (Mt 23:1-4). They retorted with an insult that showed how deeply they despised the very people they should have nurtured: "Have any of the rulers or the Pharisees believed in him? But these people who don't know the law are accursed!" (Jn 7:48-49).

So a disgraceful hiatus of pride separated the shepherds from their sheep. But in the gospel there is no such privileged class: all have the same opportunity, the same enlightenment of the Holy spirit. Now the cry goes out to all -

> *"Listen, all you who are thirsty! Here is water for you to drink! Even if you have no money, still come, buy, and eat, for you don't need any cash to buy this wine, and there is no price you could pay for this milk!" (Is 55:1).*

The gospel promise is universal, without any distinction of person of class; all may know the Lord, all may have him as their friend, all may experience his goodness, all may taste of his blessing, all may receive his reward. The Lord will teach everyone who is willing to listen how to distinguish between good and evil, how to recognise his voice, and how to run so that they are sure to win the heavenly prize.

To all, from the least to the greatest, from the noble to the most humble, there is the same promise, the same hope.

4. "I will pardon their unrighteousness, and forget their iniquity!" (vs. 12)

Is there a lovelier impulse than "mercy"? Can any sweetness surpass the experience of "pardon"? The Greek word comes from a root that means "cheerful" - so God has seen the sacrifice of his Son, found it sufficient to pay the penalty of all sin, has put away his wrath, and now looks upon us cheerfully!

The Jews used the word as an ejaculation: "Be it far from me!" Likewise, God has thrust aside our sin, and is now disposed to be kind toward us. Because of the cross he is able to forgive all the wrongdoing of those who know Jesus. Especially he is merciful to our "unrighteousness" - that is, the inbred impurity of life that stained all our actions. It describes also the non-conformity of our hearts and minds to the divine law, and the depravity of character that causes us to be mortal and corruptible. Some aspects of that unrighteousness cannot be removed until the day of resurrection, when we shall "put on incorruption and immortality"; but it has all been forgiven.

"Iniquity" includes all injustice, deviation from right living, violation of principle, crime against the law of the land, wickedness of word or deed. "Sin" means: "any voluntary transgression of the law of God; disobedience to or violation of the divine command. It includes not only actions, but neglect of known duty, all evil thoughts, words, purposes, and all that is contrary to the law of God. It may consist in commission, when a known divine law is violated; or in omission, when a positive divine command or a rule of duty is voluntarily and wilfully neglected."[23]

How rich is the Father's mercy, when it will embrace such darkness as this! Yet for all who truly repent and trust in Jesus, his promise is, "I will never again remember your sin!"

B. TIME FOR A CHANGE!

> *"When he speaks about a `new' covenant he surely makes the former covenant `old', which means that it is obsolete, decaying, ready to disappear" (vs. 13)*

---

[23] Copied from a forgotten source.

There are two words for "new" in Greek. The first means simply "new in point of time"; that is, "the latest". A car may be the latest model to come off the assembly line; it is "new", but not different from its predecessors. Then there is the word used here, which means new in every respect: new in quality, new in design, new in appearance - quite unlike anything that has gone before. So the covenant God has made with us in Christ is "new" - fresh, vital, superior. It has power also to make us "new", renewed after the likeness of Christ.

The introduction of this new covenant has made the former covenant "old" - an expression that means "cause to pass away, make obsolete". The former covenant has outlived its usefulness, it no longer has any value, its potential has been exhausted. Close examination showed that it was "decaying"; the ebbing away of its life force had brought it to the point of dissolution. It was "ready to vanish away", falling into oblivion, obliterated, abolished.

So the former covenant has been removed, and a new covenant is established in its place. We too should cast away the old and embrace the new. Have nothing more to do with the ancient regulations about days and diet, sacrifices and rituals, and righteousness based upon personal effort. Turn to Christ and rest content in the all-sufficiency of his grace! Yet we cannot abandon the old unless we first know what we are abandoning. So let us look at -

THE DESIGN OF THE OLD SANCTUARY

- see Hebrews 9:1-5

The previous chapters of Hebrews prepared the way for the theme of the next two chapters: the similarities and contrasts between the old tabernacle and its heavenly counterpart.

The apostle begins with a brief summary of some items in the tabernacle (9:1-5a). He mentions them, and leaves them, well knowing that his readers were familiar with each article and its significance: "There is no need for me to discuss these things in detail" (vs. 5b). However, today most people have little understanding of the tabernacle and its furnishings. Therefore it will be profitable for us to look more closely at this ancient sanctuary, which so vividly portrays the heavenly tabernacle.

More space is devoted to the description of the tabernacle than to any other subject in the Bible. It held immense importance as the centre of worship for the whole of Israel. It was the place of sacrifice, and the habitation in which God dwelt among his people. Neither was it of human design or origin. Seven times scripture says that Moses was commanded to make the tabernacle according to the pattern God showed him on the mountain (Ex 25:9,40; 26:20; 27:38; Nu 8:4; Act 7:44; He. 8:5). God's blueprint could not be interfered with nor altered in any way; every detail had to be strictly followed.

Why? Because, supremely, this tabernacle was a picture of the eternal things of heaven, and especially of the person and work of Christ, the Son of God. Its earthly and changing priesthood was a symbol of the unchanging Priest of Eternity.

The tabernacle did not have any great outward beauty; it was neither awe-inspiring nor graceful. But its interior splendour was breath-taking. Among structures of comparable size it may have been the most expensive ever built. Gold, silver, and precious items were lavished upon it.

It had an outer boundary that enclosed a piece of ground little bigger than the average suburban building block. This boundary was marked by sixty pillars, each a little more than 2 metres high, stayed by ropes, and standing about two metres apart. The entire area was enclosed by white linen hangings, except for an opening of four spaces at the eastern end. There the linen hangings were drawn back to form the only entrance to the main enclosure, which was known as the Outer Court.

At the eastern end of the Outer Court stood the Brazen Altar, where the sacrifices were made. Further west stood the Laver, where the priests washed themselves before entering the Holy Place.

The tabernacle itself was a tent-shaped building, located at the western end of the outer court. It was oblong, and covered by a sloping roof. Some authorities think the top was flat; but for practical reasons, relating to ease of erection and weather conditions, it seems more probable that the roof must have had at least a slight pitch.

The tabernacle was about 15 metres long, 5 metres wide, and 5 metres high. This created an area that was divided into two rooms. The only entrance, in the eastern wall, opened into the larger room (5m x 10m x 5m), known as the Holy Place. Three articles of furniture were placed there: the Table of Showbread, the Golden Candlestick and the Altar of Incense.

The second, and inner, room was known as the Holy of Holies. To the devout Israelite it was the most sacred spot on earth, and contained two vital things: the Ark of the Covenant and the Mercy Seat. Separating the two rooms was a heavy curtain known as the Veil.

Gold was lushly overlaid on all the furniture; silver ornaments abounded; the curtains were all made of the finest materials, richly dyed and magnificently embroidered. The walls consisted of gold-plated planks of acacia wood, set in silver sockets. The roof comprised four layers of cloth and leather which were draped over the walls, and on the outside fully covered them.

This all has rich meaning. Like the writer of Hebrews, I have to say that within the scope of these pages detailed explanation is not possible, but we can at least present an outline -

(1) The Outer Court opened toward the east, which reminds us of Christ, the Sun of Righteousness who will rise with healing in his rays. Only within the boundaries of this appointed sanctuary will mankind find the sunrise of a new day, the dawn of a new hope, the beginning of new life.

(2) Anyone standing outside the boundary saw only the plain linen curtains and a portion of the drab leather tent roof. Nothing of the exquisite interior was visible. So a sinner sees nothing of the beauties of the gospel, the radiant loveliness of Christian life. He sees only the linen fence, a figure of God's holiness, which bars him from entrance into the heavenly realm. He sees the outward form of spiritual things, but to him they are unattractive. The worldling may acknowledge the moral perfection of Christ, but he cannot see the Saviour's shining glory.

(3) The single entrance to the tabernacle demonstrates that there is only one way to come into the presence of God. Christ is the door.

(4) The white linen of righteousness excludes the sinner from God; but Jesus made a door in that high fence, and now all are invited to enter.

(5) The brass pillars shining against the white linen speak of God's just wrath against sinful man - condemning him to remain in the wilderness. This severe white portrays the law of God, which stands as a barrier between fallen humanity and a holy God.

(6) The curtain across the gate was made of fine white linen, with embroidered patterns of purple, scarlet, and blue. Christ is the door: purple is the sign of his royalty; scarlet, of his blood; blue, of his deity; white, of his righteousness. So they show the Saviour as King, Servant, Son of Man, and Son of God. Here we see also the four outstanding characteristics of Christ, portrayed in Ezekiel and in the four gospels as Lion, Ox, Man, and Eagle. Four is also the number of the earth, and of the family of man; hence the four openings in the gate show that all are freely invited to enter the courts of God through this door.

(7) The acacia wood used in constructing the tabernacle was a tough desert wood, which grew in the most adverse circumstances. Here we see Christ in his humanity - "He will grow before the Lord like a bush planted in a desert; so to our eyes he will seem stunted and withered, lacking any beauty that would cause us to prize him, or any charm that would make us want him" (Is 53:2).

(8) The pure gold overlay, however, speaks of the deity of Christ. The wood and the gold show his two natures, both God and man, perfectly united. Only such as he could provide a safe place where God and we sinners could meet in fellowship.

(9) There were seven articles of furniture in the tabernacle: the altar of sacrifice; the laver; the table of showbread; the candlestick; the altar of incense; the ark of the covenant; and the mercy seat. In Israel, seven was the number typical of perfection; which suggests that the tabernacle was perfect in its design, and it speaks of the perfection of him to whom those symbols point.

(10) The altar of sacrifice: the word signifies to "lift up". So was Jesus our Lamb of sacrifice lifted up on the cross. The altar stood immediately inside the main gate, demonstrating the need of sacrifice for sin before any approach to God can be made. The altar was God's design, but made by men who also lifted the sacrifices onto it. So, while God purposed for his Son to die, human hands made the cross and crucified him. Yet, even in this crime, they were providing atonement for their sins. Matchless grace of God!

The altar was equipped with two handles so that it might be easily carried from place to place. We are required to carry the cross to the ends of the earth and tell all people about the one Man who died there.

The altar had four horns, pointing to the four points of the compass - indicating power, strength, and the final universal dominion of the Lord.

The altar was made of wood, overlaid with brass, and on it the sacrifices were burnt. In this we see the body of Christ, and the judgment of God on our sins, which was expressed by his wrath poured out upon Jesus on the cross. Because of the seal of brass, the wood did not burn; so, while Christ suffered for our sins and carried our judgment, he remained unharmed, and triumphed over death.

The fire on the altar was initially kindled by God himself, and was never allowed to go out. So did Jesus once offer himself on Calvary; that sacrifice will never be repeated. At the same time, it is always efficacious; it never loses its ability to bring mercy and peace.

(11) The laver was made of solid brass and filled with water. It speaks of the Word of God, and of our need for constant "washing" in the Word, the renewal of our consecration, and the need for continual confession and cleansing. The laver was made out of brass mirrors given by the women, and so indicates the need for separation from the attractions of this world and absolute consecration to God.

The laver is the only article for which no dimensions are given; there was no set limit to its size; necessity alone determined its measure. An unlimited supply of grace to help in time of need is freely available to all who yield to God and call upon him from a sincere heart.

The tabernacle had no floor except the plain earth. The priests were therefore constantly becoming defiled, and had to resort to the laver before they could continue in their service. In this world we also come into contact with much uncleanness, which frequently leaves us stained. Only by constant recourse to the cleansing fountain can we maintain our fellowship with God.

(12) The table of showbread was made of acacia wood, overlaid with pure gold, and was about 100cm long, by 50cm wide, by 70cm deep. Fitted around its edge was a golden mounting to prevent the twelve loaves of bread from falling to the ground. The table was fitted with four golden rings to hold the staves used for carrying it.

The bread was flavoured with frankincense and reminds us of the birth of Jesus, the Bread of Heaven provided by God for the feeding of the nations. At this table the priests fellowshipped, and the bread was theirs to eat after the passing of each Sabbath. So should we gather for fellowship: daily with the Lord; and regularly with the saints, to break bread around the Lord's table. The centre of our fellowship must always be the Lord Jesus Christ, for he alone can provide all our necessary sustenance.

(13) The candlestick was the symbol of Christ, the Light of the world. A constant flow of oil fed the flame of the seven lamps, symbolic of the Holy Spirit, by whom Christ is made manifest to us. The Church also is figured here, showing that the Church, filled with the Holy Spirit, should throw a brilliant light into the darkness of this world.

(14) The altar of incense was about 100cm high, by 50cm square, made of wood and overlaid with pure gold. Here is the place of prayer, finding its ground in the humanity and the deity of Christ. We must pray in his Name, Jesus, the Name of his humanity, which is now also the exalted Name of his deity and priestly ministry.

From this altar burning incense constantly ascended before the Lord, which portrays the unceasing intercession of Christ our High Priest. The brazen altar of sacrifice prefigured the Lord's death on our behalf; the golden altar of incense prefigured his resurrection and ministry of prayer on our behalf.

This altar symbolises also the highest privilege of the believer - intercessory prayer; and it pictures the ineffable joy of our fellowship with the Father through the Son. At the "altar of incense" we draw nearest to the very heart of God, for this altar stood just outside the veil, adjacent to the holiest place, where the presence of God overshadowed the mercy seat.

(15) The veil sheltered the Holy of Holies from the rest of the tabernacle. It was a heavy embroidered curtain, which no one was allowed to pass through, on pain of death. Only the high priest was excepted, and even he only once a year, on the great Day of Atonement. The veil therefore showed that this splendid tabernacle, for all its opulence and wonderful ritual, could never really open the way for ordinary people to approach God. It always fell short of the divine ideal.

The veil especially prefigured the sinless, perfect nature of the Lord Jesus Christ. He stood in the presence of God and, by that very fact, excluded all others who were sinful and imperfect. That is, until he allowed his body to be broken - "torn in two" - and in doing so made it possible for us to assume his nature and to stand with him before the Holy God.

(16) <u>The wooden walls</u> of the inner tabernacle stood on a foundation of 100 silver sockets, which together weighed about five tonnes. This foundation, both in weight and value, seems out of proportion to the size of the building. But silver is linked in scripture with atonement (Ex 30:11-13,15) and atonement is always made by the shedding of blood. So the sockets suggested that the tabernacle rested upon a blood-foundation of immense value. Likewise, the precious blood of Christ is the foundation of our access to God; and it has an extravagant strength that goes far beyond our need.

(17) <u>The entire structure</u> was bound together with "pins" and "cords". It was so secure that for nearly 40 years it remained unmoved, unshaken even by the howling winds of the desert. Jesus provide the believer with a sure refuge, a hiding place in the storm. In Is 22:23-24, Christ is likened to a "nail" or "pin", and it is said that on him all the Father's household will be anchored. The pins were made of brass, which does not rust; and neither can our hope or safety in Christ ever fail. The pins were driven into the ground, but part of them projected from the earth so that ropes could be fastened to them; which suggests the burial and the resurrection of Christ, to which our hope of salvation is tied. The cords bound the whole structure together, holding it fast, just as the Lord draws us to himself with the strong cord of his love.

(18) <u>The roof of the tabernacle</u> proper consisted of four layers of differing material: linen; goat's hair; ram's skins; and badger's skins. <u>The linen</u> was draped over the walls first, hanging down either side. It was visible only from the inside of the tabernacle and was embroidered with blue, purple and scarlet threads. The outside view of the tabernacle showed only the drab skins, significant of the humanity and humiliation of Christ. But those who have trusted him, and entered into him, see the magnificent beauty and purity and glory of his nature.

<u>The goats' hair covering</u> was laid on top of the linen, and extended down both outer walls entirely to the ground. The goat, in the Bible, pictures Christ as our sin-bearer. Before we can know the righteousness of Christ, we must first acknowledge our sin. Reaching right to the ground, and

covering the whole tabernacle, this curtain speaks of the full shelter provided for us by Jesus' perfect sacrifice.

The third layer was made of rams' skins, dyed a deep crimson, which suggests the blood of Christ that must cover us. His blood must be our constant fount of cleansing, the mask that removes our sin from the sight of God.

The fourth cover was made from badger skins.[24] This covering was rough, drab, exposed to the wind, rain, heat, and frost. How clearly it portrays the body of Jesus' humiliation, which was cracked and broken for us, being subjected to ignominy, torture, the gaze of the vulgar.

(19) No chairs were provided in the tabernacle. The priests could never sit down, for their work was never done. We might see here two contrasting ideas:

- **first**, the insufficiency of the earthly tabernacle and its priesthood, for Christ, having offered himself once, "sat down at the right hand of the Majesty on high" - his sacrifice was eternally complete;
- **second**, the continued activity of our Great High Priest, who never rests from ministering before the Father and interceding on our behalf.

(20) The ark of the covenant was the most important item in the tabernacle and constituted the most perfect type of Christ. It was located in the Holy of Holies, which was a room approximately five metres square, and five metres in height, making a perfect cube. This reminds us of the heavenly Jerusalem, the city that is built "four-square".

The ark was an oblong box about 100cm long, by 70cm in width, and 70cm in height. Again it was made of wood, completely covered with gold, showing the deity and humanity of Jesus. Within the ark was placed the law of God, suggesting the perfect holiness and justice of Christ. Anyone who looked into the ark incurred the death penalty, for no sinful creature can behold the holy law of God and still live.

But placed on the top of the ark, and entirely covering it, was -

(21) The mercy seat. This was made of beaten gold. It sat on top of the ark, hiding the tables of the law, which spelt judgment and death. On

---

[24] Some translations prefer "porpoise skins".

this mercy seat the blood of the sacrifice was sprinkled on the day of atonement. So are we sheltered from the anger of an injured God by the shed blood of Jesus, and by his sinless life of pure gold.

(22) Also in the ark was a pot of manna, which did not rot, but was kept by God's grace and power. Jesus is the living Bread who is the eternal source of all life and strength.

(23) Included in the ark was a third item, the rod of Aaron, which God made to bud and blossom overnight. He did this to prove that Aaron was his chosen priest. It tells of resurrection, and was placed right next to the tables of the law which spoke of death. So has Christ brought life and immortality to light by the gospel.

Here we must leave this general description of the tabernacle, though what is written above has scarcely begun to unfold the depth and scope of its rich typical significance. But what has been said will provide sufficient back-ground for our continued study of the ninth chapter of Hebrews.

CHAPTER ELEVEN:

SAVIOUR

Text: Hebrews 9:1-28

The apostle describes the work of the priests in the old Jewish sanctuary, the grave defects of that ancient system, and then the glory of the new sanctuary we possess in the heavenlies. Our previous chapter began a discussion of these things, which we take up again here. But first let the apostle summarise once more the various parts of Israel's ancient tabernacle -

THE DESCRIPTION OF THE OLD SANCTUARY

> *"The first covenant had a set of regulations, which governed the divine service conducted in its man-made sanctuary. The first section of that sanctuary was an outer tent (called the Holy Place). It was built to contain the lamp stand, the table, and the sacred bread. Behind the second curtain, was another tent (called the Holy of Holies), in which stood the golden incense altar,[25] and the Ark of the Covenant. This too was plated all over with gold, and in it were kept a golden jar of manna, Aaron's staff that budded, and the two stone tablets upon which the commandments were carved. Above the ark were two winged creatures (the cherubim), who gazed down upon the place of propitiation. They symbolised the glorious presence of God. But I cannot take time now to discuss all these items in detail" (vs. 1-5).*

Some attention has already been given to the structure and furnishings of the tabernacle Moses built in the desert, and how it all relates to the gospel, so we need say no more here. Instead, let us go on to consider -

---

[25] This altar normally stood in the Holy Place, but on the Day of Atonement it was taken into the Most Holy Place, where it protected the high priest from death by filling the place with sweet smoke and so prevented him from inadvertently seeing God.

THE DEFECTS OF THE OLD SANCTUARY

A. THE DAILY MINISTRY OF THE ORDINARY PRIESTS

"In accordance with the old arrangement, the priests had to keep on going into the Holy Place, where they fulfilled their duties to God" (vs. 6)

The pattern of that first sanctuary was given by God to Moses, who built it exactly as he had been told. Then God sealed it by setting over it the pillar of cloud by day and of fire by night, which were signs of his presence among his people. The sanctuary was then ready to fulfil its purpose. So the priests walked into it, and began their daily work. Who were those priests? What was their work?

Originally the entire nation of Israel was chosen to be a kingdom of priests, serving both God and the surrounding world (Ex 19:6). But they staggered under this amazing privilege and renounced it. God complied with their choice (De 18:16-17), appointing first Moses, then the line of his brother Aaron, to become priests and mediators for Israel.

But the Lord has never lost sight of his original purpose: that his people should *all* be priests before him.[26] He has already begun to fulfil this, by nominating every believer in Christ as a priest, and adding a promise that they will reign with him as priest-kings.[27] The consummation will arrive along with the return of Christ and the inauguration of his eternal kingdom, in which Christ himself will rule as Royal High Priest, supreme in universal authority. Immediately beneath him will stand the great company of glorified saints, themselves a royal priesthood, ministering now to the entire creation.

Take notice here that the exercise of our priesthood does not await that coming day. Two of the chief functions of the priesthood are in our hands already: the privilege of offering the incense of prayer and intercession;[28] and the privilege of service and sacrifice. [29]For this reason

---

[26] See the companion book to this one "Royal Priesthood"

[27] 1 Pe 2:5,9; Re 1:6; 5:10; 20:6.

[28] Burning incense (a symbol of prayer), was always the priest's duty – 2 Ch 26:18; Ps 141:2; Re 8:3.

it is risky to call a Christian minister a "priest", as if there were some special order of priesthood established in the church, or some priestly functions that only the clergy can perform. All believers are priests; we have all been privileged with the rights of God's royal priesthood; the church in its entirety is a kingdom of priests. The pastors, the clergy, should differ from other believers only in the particular duties they are appointed to fulfil. They have no better access to the throne of God, no higher authority in the presence of God, no priestly advantage beyond what every Christian possesses.

The duties of the old priests who ministered in the outer court and in the holy place of Israel's tabernacle consisted of:

- keeping the altar fire ever burning
- replenishing the sacred lamp with oil
- staying available to serve all who came to worship God
- performing the ceremonies of purification for those who had become defiled in some way
- teaching the law to the people
- protecting the sanctuary against profanation
- blowing the silver trumpets to assemble the people
- sundry other tasks.

Those priests were all drawn from the family of Aaron, which in turn was one of the families of Levi. Hence the priests were all Levites, but not all the Levites were priests. But the entire tribe of Levi was consecrated to the service of the tabernacle. Only those Levites who were priests could make the sacrifices, burn incense, and enter into the sanctuary itself. The remaining Levites performed numerous other duties in connection with the work and ministry of the tabernacle. Both priests and Levites were supported by the tithes and offerings of the people.

Now, returning to our text, it says of the priests -

" ... they had to keep on going ..." - which speaks of their constant activity. They were to be always ready to fulfil the functions of their office, to answer the cry of any who needed their help. They were to be found working diligently at their proper tasks at the appointed times. So strict was this demand that they were forbidden to mourn for any but

---

[29] The false priest fattens himself upon the sacrifices of the people; the true priest sacrifices himself in the service of the people (Ez 34:1-21).

their closest relatives. They constitute a strong type of the consecration, devotion, and unwearied activity that the Lord expects from us now -

> *"Christ sacrificed himself for us to redeem us from all iniquity, so that we might be his very own people, eager to work hard in his service" (Tit 2:14).*

" ... into the sanctuary ..." To minister effectively, the priests had to stand in the presence of God, washed, purified, wholly consecrated to his will, having no desire to mix carnal things with divine service.

" ... into the Holy Place ..." They were forbidden on pain of death to enter the Holy of Holies (the innermost part of the tabernacle), just as the ordinary people were forbidden to enter the Holy Place. Such provisions show that no one should take upon themselves any function in the church unless God has called them and ordained them to it. Even ministers have their proper place and should not try to go beyond the service appointed for them by God.

" ... fulfilled their duties to God ..." The apostle does not doubt that the ancient sanctuary and its priestly service were set up in obedience to the will of God. They became obsolete only after the heavenly pattern was fulfilled in Christ. So in their rituals and ceremonies, in their sacrifices and prayers, the priests were doing the Lord's work, and his blessing was added to it. Further, they "fulfilled their task, labouring until every duty was done, and every requirement satisfied. May the Lord help us to do the same!

B. THE ANNUAL MINISTRY OF THE HIGH PRIEST

1. The Great Day of Atonement

> *"Once every year, the high priest went alone into the Holy of Holies. He had to take with him the blood, which he presented on his own behalf, and for the faults of the people" (vs. 7)*

Now the apostle turns to one of the most important days in Israel's sacred year, the Day of Atonement (see Le 23:26-32), in which the high priest performed the sacrifices that were required to expiate his own sins and those of the entire nation.

This annual event occurred on the tenth day of the seventh month, which Jewish tradition held to be the exact anniversary of the day when Adam and Eve violated God's order and ate the forbidden fruit.

Just as atonement was made for Israel on this set day, once in every year, so Christ died once at the appointed time in the "year" of eternity.

This day contrasted sharply with other sacred days in Israel's calendar. They were occasions for song and dance, but this was marked by sorrow and fasting. Their sound was melody and laughter, this was lamentation and ashes. Their focus was praise and thanksgiving, this was confession and repentance. The demand made by God was stringent: the people had to concentrate upon this day; they were forbidden to do any work; nothing must be allowed to distract their attention from the duty of afflicting their souls. They were to see and know fully the awful hiatus created between heaven and earth by human sin, and that only a God-approved sacrifice could fill that dread chasm.

The fasting portrayed the suffering that inescapably arises from sin. The sacrifice showed God's estimate of the vileness of sin, and it pointed also to the one perfect sacrifice of Christ. The penalty that fell heavily upon those who refused to observe this day suggests the eternal judgment that will punish those who reject the atonement made by Christ.

2. *The Cleansing of the Altar and People*

See Le 16:29-34. Here we find the purpose of the Day of Atonement: "that in the sight of God, you may all be clean of sin." Atonement was made for the sanctuary, the tabernacle, the altar, the high priest, the ordinary priests, the people, and for the entire land - for sin had contaminated them all.

In English, the basic meaning of "atonement" is simply to be "at-one-with", and it suggests the idea of a sinner being brought into perfect one-ness with God. But that would be a misleading meaning to give to the Hebrew word, which conveys more the image of a "covering". If the levitical sacrifices secured pardon for Israel, they did so only in the shadow of the cross. Whatever strength they possessed depended upon the then still future sacrifice made by Christ. In reality, the offerings of the first tabernacle could provide only a "covering" for sin, they were powerless to remove it, or to break its grip, or to bring the sinner into full communion with the Father. Only the cross is mighty enough to work such miracles.

3. *The Task of the High Priest*

(a) Please read Le 16:1-34. Once a year, and only once, the high priest was allowed to walk into the Holy of Holies, and there make atonement for himself and his people. The death penalty was attached to any deviation from the rigid procedures established in the law of Moses. Even after the most rigorous attention to detail, the high priest would still enter with fear and trembling, lest the Almighty should refuse to accept him. What a contrast with the Lord Jesus, who entered the holiest with boldness, and sat down with confidence at the right hand of God!

(b) Note that while death threatened the high priest every time he entered the Holy of Holies, death threatens us if we fail to go in there, and that constantly! (He 10:20).

(c) Tradition says that the high priest had to prepare himself for seven days, studying the scriptures, practising the ritual, making himself thoroughly familiar with every part of the ceremony. Then, on the Day of Atonement itself, he performed, by himself, all the ordinary duties of the temple, leading up to the special ceremonies and the immolation of the animal sacrifices. Similarly, so that he might perfectly fulfil the ancient type, Jesus too had to "learn obedience", and he was "made perfect by the things he suffered" (He 5:8-9).

(d) Before he could make atonement for the nation, Aaron had to present a sin-offering for himself and for his house (Le 16:6). He took off the gorgeous ceremonial robes that were the badge of his office, washed himself from head to toe, and put on simple garments, made of pure white linen. Washed and attired, he then offered his own bullock to the Lord, acknowledging that although he was God's chosen priest he was also one with the fallen nation. Just as Aaron so identified himself with his people, Jesus united himself with us. This process began with his birth, but was publicly avowed when he allowed John to baptise him in the Jordan. Jesus too, presented himself as a sin-offering to the Father - although not for himself (as Aaron had to do), but for the people. This difference was marked at his baptism. Matthew tells us that the people stood in the river, "confessing their sins"; but Jesus, after his baptism, "went up at once out of the water" (Mt 3:6,16). He had no sin to confess; his baptism was solely one of identification with the people in their sin.

(e) After he had everything ready to make atonement for the sins of his own family, Aaron was then free to act on behalf of the nation. He took two goats. They were both presented before the Lord, and then one was chosen by lot to be a sin-offering. This was known as the offering "for the Lord"; the other was called the "scape-goat". Using a lot to choose the role of each goat demonstrated God's inalienable right to decide the proper sacrifice for sin. So he did when he chose Christ, and none may choose another.

(f) Now Aaron proceeded to offer his own bullock. It was killed, then left on the altar while Aaron took a golden censer of incense and, reaching his hand through the veil, filled the Holy of Holies with fragrant smoke. He had to obscure the ark of the covenant and to dim the brilliance of the shekinah - the glory of God that shone between the cherubim. Only then was it safe for him to take the blood of his sin-offering and sprinkle it on the mercy seat (the golden lid of the ark), thus making atonement for his sin. Some lessons come out of this:

- the weakness of the levitical system, because it gave only a restricted and clouded view of God
- by prayer (incense) alone are we able to enter into the holiest
- by contrast with Aaron, Christ our High Priest looks upon the Father face to face and does not flinch from that ineffable splendour, for he is himself the "radiance of God's glory, the express likeness of his person" (He 1:3).

(g) The goat for the sin-offering was now killed and its blood sprinkled around the sanctuary (Le 16:15-19). The unavoidable corruption sin brings, and the ultimate failure of the old earthly tabernacle is shown by this: the holy things themselves had to be cleansed, for even they were polluted.

During these ministrations, no one except the high priest was permitted to enter the sanctuary (vs. 17). Jesus also stood alone when he sacrificed his life and made atonement for us -

> "I trod the winepress alone; and there was no one among the people who stood with me ... By himself he made atonement for our sin" (Is 63:3; He 1:3).

(h) The first goat was forced to accept the penalty for the nation's sin: death. But then the scapegoat was brought forward. Its task was to carry all their iniquity right out of the camp.

> *"Aaron must lay both his hands upon the head of the scapegoat, and confess over it all the sins, wickedness, and disobedience of the people of Israel. By his hands he will transfer these evils to the goat's head. Then he will put the goat into the charge of a man who is fit, ready, and waiting. That man must lead the goat out into the desert, and there release it, where no human lives. The goat must carry the sins of the people into an uninhabited wilderness" (Le 16:21-22).*

Just as the scapegoat was sent into the desert on the tenth day of the seventh month, so Jesus, we are told, went "outside the camp", and was crucified, and buried there, and carried our unrighteousness far away.

> *"As far as the east is from the west, so far has he removed our transgressions from us" (Ps 103:12).*

> *"The Lord will turn toward us again, he will show us mercy, he will crush our iniquities, he will throw all our sins to the bottom of the deepest sea" (Mi 7:19)*

According to some traditions, after Solomon had built the temple in Jerusalem, it became the practice for the "fit man" (how vividly is Jesus the true Man portrayed) to take the scapegoat, bind a scarlet ribbon around its neck, and pull it through the great congregation gathered in the temple court. As the poor, terrified, bleating beast was dragged past them, the people wept and moaned for their guilt, striving to touch the beast and to cast their sins upon it. Eventually arriving at an appointed spot in the wilderness, the man threw the animal over a cliff to its death on the rocks below. As the goat fell, he kept his eye fixed on the ribbon, for it was said that if the Lord had accepted their offering, and had pardoned the people, the scarlet would become snow white. When he observed the change, and saw the animal dead, the man rushed back to the temple shouting with joy. When the people heard his good news, they too began to laugh and sing, to dance and worship, until the whole city echoed with their gladness. Their sins were gone!

Surely Isaiah had such images in mind when he wrote -

"Come now," says the Lord, "and let us argue this matter together: even if your sins are stained scarlet, they will be white as snow; though they are red as crimson, they will become like wool ... His appearance was so marred, he no longer looked human; his form was so broken, he lost the shape of a man ... Surely he bore our pains and carried our diseases. At first we thought that his blows and sufferings were a punishment from God. But he was wounded for our wrongdoing; he was beaten for our iniquity; he was flogged so that we might be forgiven; and his scars are the mark of our healing" (Is 1:18; 52:14; 53:3-5).

(i) When the ceremonies were completed, the high priest put off his linen garments, resumed his splendid robes, and then offered a ram as a burnt offering (Le 16:5,24). This was a consecration offering, whereby the people dedicated themselves anew to God.

4. The Purpose of the Holy Spirit

So we have an outline of the salient features of the Day of Atonement. Those are the things alluded to in He 9:7. Notice again:

- as the high priest alone could enter the Holiest, which is a symbol of heaven, so Christ alone had the right to approach the supernal throne, and he not by a legal statute, but by his own merit.
- to enter the Holiest, Aaron had to pass through the Outer Court and the Holy Place; so Jesus had to pass through a human and a holy life.
- the high priest entered annually, his work never completed; but Christ has entered once for all.
- without blood the high priest dared not enter the Holiest; so Christ bore with him his own precious blood; and neither may we enter the Holiest except we carry upon us the mark of that same blood.

"By all of these things," said the apostle, "the Holy Spirit was clearly showing that, so long as the old sanctuary stood, the way into the Holy of Holies was not yet open. It was at best a symbol that pointed to the present time" (He 9:8,9).

The old sanctuary prevented all but the high priest from getting access to the Holiest. The glory of the inner sanctum was hidden, its power remained veiled. So while the tabernacle in the desert did point the way to God, it nonetheless barred ordinary men and women from God. It was but a symbol of the heavenly reality, pointing toward the time when that reality would be unveiled. Divorced from that reality, the former sanctuary had no lasting value. While it was a divinely appointed structure, in which "both gifts and sacrifices were offered", it remained evident that those gifts did not even reach God, since they were consumed by the priests; and the sacrifices, while they were meant to atone for sin, were themselves ritually unclean, since those who touched them had to be ceremonially washed before they could re-enter the congregation.

So the temple ordinances "were incapable either of giving worshippers a clear conscience or of bringing them to perfection". Even if devout people observed every detail of the levitical system, still their consciences were left unsatisfied, still they were plagued by guilty fears, still they had to return year after year to repeat the sacrifices. In fact, the more piously they kept the rituals, the more strongly the inadequacy of those ceremonies was forced upon them. Each deepening of their moral awareness led to an increasing discontentment with the blood of beasts. They were locked into a dilemma: conscience drove them to sacrifice at the altar; but then that same conscience would condemn the offerings as unworthy!

The animal sacrifices of the old order were unable to ease a troubled conscience because, though they could not cleanse or renew the soul of the worshipper, still they aroused a sense of the sinfulness of sin. They pointed to God's requirement of moral perfection, but could not help anyone to achieve that goal because they were themselves imperfect.

Further, how could such ultimately trivial "external regulations, dealing only with food and drink and various washings," have any effect upon matters of the human spirit. Such rules could never do anything more than control bodily behaviour; they were helpless to reshape a person's inner life. They were imposed upon Israel only as a temporary measure "until God's new order came into being" (vs. 10). The apostle uses a strong word, which I have translated "imposed". Those ancient ordinances were an imposition; failure to observe them carried grievous physical penalties; constant fear was involved in their use - even the high priest trembled in terror of death as he entered the Holy of Holies.

"But then Christ came!" (vs. 11). A "new order" was inaugurated. The literal meaning of the original is "a time of thorough straightening" - that is, a time when the approach to God has been made plain and clear, a line so uncluttered that even a little child can follow it. The gospel rectifies all the defects of the old way. In God's new and better sanctuary a better sacrifice has been established. The conscience finds true peace. Perfection is now freely offered to all.

CHAPTER TWELVE:

FULFILLER

Text: Hebrews 9:11-14

Once again we pick up the theme of the remarkable ninth chapter of Hebrews. But for a moment, let us go back to the first verse -

> *"The former covenant had a set of regulations that governed the divine service conducted in its man-made sanctuary."*

As we have seen, this part of Hebrews presents a series of contrasts between the heavenly pattern and its earthly copy. Now the first covenant had sundry rules that governed its order of service, and it had a divinely ordained sanctuary. That sanctuary was diminished by the earthly materials from which it was made; nonetheless it deserved the highest honour -

(1) It contained "regulations"; that is, "deeds of equity ... right statutes ... true decisions ... acts of justification". These rules and principles were all prescribed by the direct authority of God, and were binding upon the whole nation.

(2) It established a "divine service", a ministry that brought reconciliation and peace, a form of worship that was acceptable to God, and which alone bore the seal of divinity.

(3) It provided a "sanctuary", a place of shelter, comfort, worship, peace, and the presence of God.

But it remained in the end a "man-made" sanctuary. This fixed its limits, exposed its temporary nature, and decreed its eventual decay. So God had to find a way to give his people access to the heavenly sanctuary, of which the desert tabernacle was but a poor copy.

That brings us to our present text, and to the joyful task of unpacking one of the richest passages in Hebrews. Our previous chapter, you may recall, had two main headings -

The Description of the Old Sanctuary

The Defects of the Old Sanctuary

- now we continue our quest with this heading -

THE DISCLOSURE OF THE NEW SACRIFICE

A. THE PERFECT SANCTUARY

"But now, Christ has come! He is the high priest of good things that are already here, and he serves in a greater and more perfect sanctuary, one that is not man-made, nor is it of this world" (vs. 11)

The passage begins with a dramatic phrase that stands at the divide of history, separating all that is old from all that is new: *"**Christ has come!**"* How much is expressed in those words! In him the times of reformation began, and still continue!

The Saviour has become *"the High Priest of the good things that are now available."* Every blessing promised in the temple, but not fulfilled, is now open to us in Christ. "Good" means complete, perfect, desirable, full, useful, valuable, kind, pleasant - and all these are applicable to the gospel and to the riches that accrue to us from the ministry of our great High Priest. So we may boldly affirm that

- our hope in him is a valid hope; it will never fail
- the promise of the gospel stands firm and sure upon the oath of God
- there is nothing weak or defective in the new covenant; it has adequate strength to supply our every need, to support us in every trial
- it has the qualities that are best adapted to comfort and remove all human ills; its blessings are eminently desirable; it will never fail to perform its promise.

How did this come about? The high priest of old entered the Holy of Holies by passing through the Holy Place. But by the pathway of his own flesh Jesus entered the Holiest in heaven, that "greater and more perfect sanctuary", not made by human hands nor constructed from earthly materials. See the description of this which far surpasses anything said of the temple -

"The Word became a man, and he lived among us. We gazed upon his glory, and saw the splendour of the Father's only Son, full of grace and truth" (Jn 1:14)

By our union with him through faith, we have now become *"members of his body"*, and so in him we too have access into the very presence of God, and that without any fear. What happiness is here! Through the broken body of Jesus, now raised and glorified, we share the supernal privilege of standing closest to heaven's throne, closer even than the mighty seraphim, having full access to every blessing that lies in the Father's love.

B. THE PERFECT SACRIFICE

"Christ entered once into the Holy of Holies, not by the blood of goats and calves, but by his own blood. There he has now obtained for us eternal freedom and life." *(He 9:12)*

The ministry of Jesus our High Priest is not expressed through the blood of goats and calves, animals that are less in value than a human being, beasts that are innocent only because they are not capable of moral fault. Neither does he enter into the Holiest by the slaughter of such creatures, nor does he attempt to secure reconciliation between us and God by the presentation of their blood. No, in place of the blood of an animal, he gave his own life; in place of the life of a brute beast, he offered his own blood. The apostle emphasises this: *it was his own blood.* It was his to give or to with-hold; no one could take his life from him. It was his own blood, therefore it was his life, for (as scripture says) *"the life is in the blood"*. It was his blood, therefore precious beyond compare, utterly pure, infinitely valuable.

Proof that his blood had been shed, and his life offered, lay in the wounds he carried into the heavenlies at his ascension, and showed to the Father. By the limitless merit of that sacrifice he was able to go in his humanity into the most interior parts of heaven's glory, there to stand in intercession for his people. There he at once began his ministry of priestly service at the throne, entreating the mercy, grace, and help of God for all who call upon his name.

He entered *"once"* - that is, once for all. He has passed into the Holiest, and he will now never leave it. Our High Priest entered there once for all time, once for all believers, once for all sin. The result? He has "*obtained for us eternal freedom and life*". When something is "obtained" there must have been an expenditure of special effort, of toil, or sacrifice. So, at the enormous cost of his own life blood - he could pay no higher price - the Lord of glory has gained full possession of everlasting redemption. It belongs now solely to him, to dispose of as he will. Being tender and kind, full of mercy and compassion, he has made this possession over to us. he obtained it not for his own benefit, but for ours. He requires only that we should gratefully acknowledge his gift, and receive it with joyful thanksgiving.

We may well be filled with gratitude and praise, for this gift may also be called an "*eternal ransoming*" (lit.). When a person is ransomed, he is released from captivity or bondage in response to some payment. A ransom price is the sum of money required to liberate a slave and to restore him to freedom and happiness. A ransom may also be paid to regain goods that were captured by an enemy. What value must the blood of Jesus have held, for it has secured an eternal ransom for every person who is enslaved by sin and death! But if a person prefers captivity to liberty, if he likes chains better than freedom, and death more than life, then the ransom price is made void. It is effective only for those who gleefully grasp their deliverance in Christ. For them his precious blood avails to redeem them from all bondage, to loose them from every fetter, to buy them out of their slavery, and to free them from the penalty of their sin. Jesus bore our punishment; he gained our pardon.

It is perhaps wise to add that, while our ransom price could be nothing less than the precious blood of the spotless Lamb of God, shed to release us from the grip of Satan, that priceless treasure was certainly not paid to the devil. He had authority over us only so long as the law of God was being violated. Therefore the blood of Jesus was presented to God in expiation for that broken law, which then closed to Satan his right to accuse and afflict those who had sinned.

C. THE PERFECT SANCTIFICATION

> "*The blood of bulls and goats, and the ashes of a heifer, sprinkled upon an unclean person, were treated by God as if they were enough to wash away defilement and to make the offender ritually holy*" (vs. 13).

Under the old covenant the blood of certain animals was reckoned sufficient to wash away any kind of outer defilement. These sacrifices achieved a cleansing from ceremonial impurity, they took away the threat of temporal punishment, and they brought some external benefit and reward. So the blood of the bullock purified Aaron, freeing him to minister in the Holy of Holies without risk of being destroyed by the holy wrath of God. Similarly, the blood of the goat removed guilt from the people, and outwardly purified the nation in the sight of God (Le 16:6,16). And the ashes of a heifer purged individuals who had become ritually defiled in some way (Nu 19:9,17-18).

But none of those offerings could touch the deeply rooted principle of sin, the corrupted nature, with which every person is born They could not really cleanse anyone; they could not create the kind of dynamic holiness that would enable a former sinner to stand unashamed in the presence of the Lord God.

This brings us to the second stage of our Christian walk. We begin by discovering forgiveness, our first redemption, through faith in the atoning work of Christ. But then we need to enter into a continuing process of cleansing that will enable us to walk in happy harmony with our Lord. The word that expresses this is "sanctification", which means to "make holy", to "separate", to "set apart" for the service of God. We all need to be thus purified, prepared for the Master's work, made able to receive his goodness and his gifts.

This deeper "sanctification" was prefigured by the "ritual holiness" mentioned in our text above, and especially in the "ashes of a heifer" (Nu 19:1-10,17-18). Here is a picture of how the sacrifice of Christ provides a fountain of cleansing from the defilement we all fall into day by day. Here also is illustrated the method by which we gain victory over the temptations that lead to sin.

1. *The Ashes of a Heifer*

The heifer was chosen with more care than was devoted to any other sacrifice. Diligent search had to be made for "*a red heifer without blemish or defect, one that has never worn a yoke*". When a suitable beast was found it was then killed and burnt. Unlike all the others, this sacrifice was not constantly repeated, for after the animal was burnt its ashes were kept and then used in future purification ceremonies. All of this speaks of Christ, who alone was the one complete sacrifice, who died once to redeem all.

The heifer had to be "*red*". The Jews said that if so much as two hairs were black or white the sacrifice was unlawful. Such an animal would have been rare; indeed, there may have been only one in all their herds. Christ is the "*fairest of ten thousand*", with whom none can be compared. Being red, the heifer typified Christ as the last Adam,[30] who was "*red in his apparel*" (Is 63:2), and was made red with his own blood.

The heifer had to be one that had "*never worn a yoke*", in which we see the voluntary offering of Jesus. He was drawn to the cross only by the compulsion of love.

The heifer was to be provided at the expense of the entire congregation, for they all stood to benefit by its death, just as we also, all of us, benefit from Christ. Now notice –

(a) The heifer was taken outside the camp, and killed in the presence of the high priest. So was Christ our perfect sacrifice, put to death at Calvary before the gaze of the assembled priests, and in the sight of God.

(b) The blood of the heifer was then sprinkled seven times before the sanctuary, thus typifying the entire, once-for-all, acceptable sacrifice of Christ. By this sacrifice the believer's sin is removed far away; and, just as the blood was taken and sprinkled around the sanctuary by the finger of the high priest, so are we brought again into fellowship with God through the merit of Calvary's Victim.

(c) The slaughtered heifer was then burnt, along with some pieces of cedar, hyssop, and scarlet - which were used in the ritual for lepers (Le 14:6-7), showing that healing of sickness as well as pardon for sin are provided for in the atonement. These items were to be thoroughly burnt, reduced entirely to ashes, which reminds us of the total consecration Christ made of himself to suffering and death, holding back nothing of himself, so that we might be fully saved.

(d) The ashes were then carefully gathered and kept in store. Whenever someone needed to be ceremonially purified, a pinch of the ashes was mixed with water and sprinkled upon that person. Hence the

---

[30] "Adam" means "red", the colour of the earth.

ashes of the one heifer were enough to serve Israel for a long time, which again shows the eternal efficacy of the one sacrifice of Christ.

The preserved ashes were a memorial of the heifer that had died, and they had to be kept in a ceremonially clean place. For us the parallel is found in the eucharist, where we are instructed to break bread in remembrance of Christ, confident that we will be purified from all defilement. We are also warned that we must keep the feast with a "clean" heart, that is, in a worthy manner, otherwise we shall succeed only in eating and drinking ourselves into the judgment of God (1 Co 11:23-33).

Note that ashes may be kept indefinitely without corruption; they suffer no change across the passage of many years. Neither does the memorial feast of the church ever lose its freshness or vitality for those who there love to meet the Lord; neither does the value of the blood of Christ ever diminish; neither does the strength of his atonement ever change; neither will it ever fail to effect purification in the lives of those who trust in him.

(e) The ashes of the heifer were applicable not only to Israelites, but also to *"every foreigner who lives among you"*, which points to the universal benefit, sufficient for all nations and generations, of the death of Christ.

(f) That the sacrifice of the heifer was only a type, pointing to a better reality, is shown by the ceremonial defilement of all who touched it (Nu 19:7-8,10). It was said by the Jews that this was a mystery that defied even the wisdom of Solomon: how the same thing could *pollute* those that were clean, but *purify* those who were unclean! But in all these things the Holy Spirit was showing that a better sacrifice was yet to come.

2. The Purifying of the Saints

In the ritual of the heifer there is an illustration of how we who become stained by sin from time to time may be purified and restored to fellowship with the Father. When conviction of sin comes upon us, and our joy in Christ is dimmed, we should not despair, but remember instead that all the guilt of sin was borne away by Christ on the cross. Quickly confess your sin, therefore, and throw your faith onto the blood of Jesus, trusting him to secure your pardon and purification.

There are two aspects of sin: guilt; and defilement. Both are removed by the grace of God, which is pictured in the water and the ashes. The ashes speak of the sacrifice that provides pardon; the water of the blood that provides purification. Christ is the source of forgiveness and of freedom.

Also in the ashes and the water there is an illustration of the way to avoid being trapped by sin. The ashes are akin to the bread of the eucharist, the memorial of the Saviour's broken body; and the water speaks of his word, in which we should constantly "bathe" ourselves. Regular observance of the Lord's Supper, and continual absorption of God's word, provide strong weapons against Satan's attacks. Unlike the old practices, which offered nothing better than "ritual holiness", these powerfully sanctify us entirely, body, soul, and spirit, making us holy through and through!

D. THE PERFECT SERVICE

> *"What great power the blood of Christ has! Through the eternal Spirit he offered himself as an unblemished sacrifice to God, so that now he can relieve your conscience from the burden of your dead works and release you to serve the living God" (He 9:14)*

The ancient sacrifices at least achieved this: "they were sufficient to achieve ritual holiness"; or, to put it another way, they "achieved enough sanctification to purify the flesh". What then will not the blood of Christ achieve? For it is said -

(1) **"Christ offered himself"**. He came to Calvary voluntarily, freely, and fully. The beasts of old were dragged unwillingly to the altar; with loud bellows and struggles they resisted the knife that drew off their life's blood. But Jesus made no defiance. He might have called upon twelve legions of angels, but instead quietly yielded himself to the cruelty and bitter hatred of those who slew him.

(2) Christ offered himself *"through the eternal Spirit"*. We can see here two things. First: the beasts of old were dragged by the priests to the altar, but Jesus was led and upheld by the eternal Spirit. Second, it refers to the infinite value of his sacrifice, for it was because of his pre-existent, divine personality that he was able to offer himself as an unblemished and entirely sufficient sacrifice. His was also an offering without fault, which could never be said of any beast. Even though the

most diligent search might fail to reveal a flaw, the piercing eye of God would yet discover many an imperfection, many a mark that showed the animal was less than exemplary.

But with Christ, both heaven and earth declared him faultless; for even Pilate said, "I find no wrong in him;" and God said, "*This is my beloved Son, with whom I am very pleased!*"

(3) The purpose of Christ's offering himself was that "*his blood might relieve your conscience from the burden of your dead works and release you to serve the living God.*" The blood of Christ releases us from the need to keep the lifeless observances of the law. Those were truly "*dead works*", based on inanimate objects, driven by a lifeless commandment. They also brought death, because, although they demanded perfection, they gave no help toward that goal. Rather, they increased the heavy load of guilt, they burdened the soul with chains of legal minutiae.

How different the result of Calvary! What deep peace arises from the blood of the cross! All inward accusation falls quiet; silence marks the once-clamorous voice of conscience. The blood of Jesus reaches deep into the soul, carrying away all sin, obliterating all guilt, cleansing all stain. The gospel pushes aside those old carnal rites that dealt only *with "food and drink, and various ceremonial washings.*" They were all "*external ordinances, useful only until the new era arrived*" (9:10). Now they are superfluous, foreign to the ways of the Spirit of God.

Does this mean we can whatever we like? Hardly! We are released from the suffocating grip of conscience so that we might serve God in the freedom of new-born children. Christ looses our heavy burdens so that we might minister before him with joy, and worship him with gladness. Could we do any other? The sense of guilt, the defilement that once separated us from God and made us fearful of his presence, has vanished! Now we are clothed with holiness, sanctified by his strong hand, fit to stand tall at his throne, and able to "*serve the living God*".

Never again think to please him by the performance of "*dead works*", but rather by a life renewed and quickened by the Holy Spirit, standing in the grace of Christ.

THE DEDICATION OF THE NEW SANCTUARY

- see Hebrews 9:15-22

"For this cause" (to purge and purify people to serve the living God) Jesus became the negotiator of an entirely new agreement, set out in the form of a will. The benefit promised in this will was *"an eternal inheritance"* (vs. 15). But before any will can become effective the death of the testator must be established (vs. 16). No will has any force while the one who made it is still alive (vs. 17). The death of Jesus, the author of the will, was therefore necessary before anyone could receive its promise of eternal inheritance. But another difficulty then appears: how can a sinful people receive such an inheritance? This was overcome by the redemption that was also created by Jesus' death, as we have seen. So the Lord made a promise, incorporated it in a *"will"*, and then died to bring his will into effect. Then he rose again to the right hand of God so that he might himself become the Mediator, the Executor, of that will and disperse its largess to all the beneficiaries. How marvellous then is the grace of God! How wonderful the plan of redemption!

By his death, Christ has provided rescue from all the transgressions that we have committed against the Ten Commandments and the laws that sprang from them. Further, by his death, Christ has created an inheritance for us: that is, an estate in heaven, which becomes the freehold possession of every believer, received by gift. To this inheritance we have an absolute title, so that it becomes the permanent, eternal property of all who walk in righteous fellowship with their Lord.

The apostle then reverts to the old order again to show how these principles applied there. He says: "Note that even the first covenant had to be dedicated with blood" (vs. 18). By the spilling of blood it was inaugurated; by the shedding of blood it was ratified; without the constant flow of blood it had no force. Here again the two-fold purpose of the victim's death is revealed: to make the provisions of the testament effective; and to purge those who are to receive those benefits. Watch Moses begin the process -

> *"Moses told the people all the instructions contained in the law; then he took the blood of calves and goats, along with water, scarlet wool, and hyssop, and sprinkled both the book, and all the people. Then he*

said, `This is the blood of the covenant that God has commanded you to keep'" (vs. 19-21).

The "blood and water" suggest the blood and water that poured from the Saviour's side: the blood for our justification; the water for our sanctification. The scarlet wool speaks of the righteousness of Christ, out of which wool our garments must be made, the only garments that can hide our nakedness. The hyssop speaks of the faith that gives force to the words of the Book - faith without which "it is impossible to please God" (He 11:6).

Moses applied the blood to the Book and to the people. The blood is effective only when it is applied, and the words of the Book hold only for those who are sanctified by the blood. How vital then that we should hold onto the blood of Christ, actively applying it to our lives each day, constantly seeing it with the eye of faith.

To show that all those old ordinances were actually ineffective, the Spirit of God then directed Moses to sprinkle the sanctuary and all its vessels, thus marking the uncleanness of even those holy objects. The effect should have been to turn the eyes of the people toward sun, of which these things were only the shadow. But they were blind and refused to see. However, we may learn that our own worship and ministry, and those things we use in the service of God, will be accepted by the Lord only as by faith we keep them sprinkled with the blood of Christ.

Finally, he says: "Under the law virtually everything must be purged with blood; indeed, without shedding of blood no remission of sin occurs." What was true then remains true of the heavenly sanctuary: only by the blood of Christ is it possible to find release from the guilt of sin, pardon from the merited punishment of sin, and strength to conquer the habit of sin. For all those things, and more, his blood is entirely sufficient!

THE DIVERGENCE OF THE TWO SANCTUARIES

- see Hebrews 9:23-28

A. THE CONTRAST IN PURITY

"If those things that were only copies of the heavenly reality had to be purged by these rituals, then the

heavenly things must require a far better sacrifice (vs.23)

The old tabernacle had to be purified, because it was only an earthly copy of the heavenly original. Being an earthly building, it was purified with earthly things. Yet how impure was its purity when those who came into contact with it were themselves made unclean!

Now compare this with the heavenly altar, which was so free of corruption that it demanded an infinitely superior sacrifice. The earthly altar required a sacrifice to purify it, but could find nothing better than an impure animal. But the heavenly altar was already supremely pure and would tolerate nothing less than an utterly pure sacrifice. In the Son of God alone was one found who was able to present himself as that better and nobler Victim.

B. THE CONTRAST IN PRESENCE

"Christ did not go into some man-made holy place, which at best was a copy of the true sanctuary; instead he has gone into heaven itself, where he now speaks for us in the presence of God" (vs. 24).

The apostle carries his thought further: Christ is a Sacrifice whose glory surpasses even that of the sanctuary, though it is the very the sanctuary that enshrines the presence of God. How different this is from the old tabernacle! That was made by human hands, which proved its temporary nature, its inability to provide an eternal redemption; but this is found in heaven itself, and can never be destroyed.

For a few brief moments, the high priest of old stood trembling in the smoke-filled Holy of Holies, quickly sprinkled a few drops of blood on the clouded mercy seat and hastily left the room, not to return for another twelve months. But Jesus entered into the highest heaven, there to remain, and there to speak continually for us in the presence of God. There he sits in majesty at the right hand of God. There he acts as our representative, presenting our prayers to the Father, securing our welfare, rebuking our accuser, and gaining us mercy and grace. There he is gathering our reward, and preparing the place to which he will bring us on that great coming day!

C. THE CONTRAST IN PRIESTHOOD

> *"Unlike the high priest, who had to go into the Holiest every year with blood (although not his own), Jesus does not keep on offering himself, for that would mean he had suffered countless times since the world began. Rather, he appeared once for all at the end of the age to abolish sin by the sacrifice of himself" (vs. 25-26)*

The high priest of old went into the Holiest every year, year in and year out, carrying blood that was "not his own". It was the blood of beasts that were different in nature and character from the people who needed pardon. Plainly, such sacrifices, of creatures whose value was slight, could never truly obliterate the sin of a morally accountable and rational human being. The apostle has raised this point before. Why does he mention it again? Apparently to anticipate some who might object that one sacrifice (as of Christ) could not possibly be continually effective. He replies, first, by showing the necessity of a better sacrifice than that of beasts; and second, by insisting that Christ's one offering is both nobler and sufficient -

> *"Jesus could not keep on making himself a victim, for then he must often have suffered since the foundation of the world."*

Christ is High Priest of the heavenly sanctuary, a sanctuary which, as we have seen, existed from the beginning of the time, and which had an altar (like all altars) that required a sacrifice. If his one offering was not sufficient to reach back into all the past and forward into all the future, the impossible situation of the Son of God having to suffer, die, and rise again continually would arise. That could never be. Now we realise why Jesus was willing to make himself the sacrifice for sin: in all the universe he alone had within himself sufficient value to make a "once for all" atonement.

So it is said: "He appeared <u>once</u> at the end of the age." He came as a man, clothed in mortal garb, stripped of the outward form of his deity. The Son of God appeared once in this manner, but never again will he so appear. When the world next sees him, it will be in his glory.

But, in that first coming, he demonstrated his greater Priesthood by "obliterating sin by the sacrifice of himself". When Jesus died, he grasped hold of sin, crushed it, cast it away, demolished it. It is now as though it had never been! Dare to reckon this true of your own life! Is your sin greater than Christ? Can it go beyond the love of Christ? Can it master the mercy of God? Jesus was one with God, and he sacrificed himself for you. Sin is put away! Once and for all! Believe it and receive it!

D. THE CONTRAST IN POWER

> *"Just as it is appointed for every person to die once, and after that comes the judgment, so Christ, having offered himself once for the sins of the people, will come a second time - not to deal with sin, but to bring salvation to those who are eagerly looking for him!" (vs. 27-28)*

The dismal first covenant could offer no better than this: a lonely passage through death, and the certain judgment that would follow. The ordinances, the laws, the rituals, of the old covenant ended by showing us our sin, and the wrath of God against sin. Not so the new covenant which has in it the power of salvation. Now see -

1. The Two Appointments of God for Mankind

We are appointed to die and, having died, cannot return to undo those things we have done. It therefore behoves us to live well that we might also die well.

We are appointed to judgment. There is a judgment that takes place immediately after death, a separation of the righteous from the unrighteous. The unjust are reserved under punishment, awaiting the final Day of Judgment and their eternal sentence (2 Pe 2:9). The just rest in the presence of the Lord, awaiting the day of resurrection and their eternal reward.

At the end of the ages there will come the great Day of Judgment, at the Great White Throne of God, when all people will finally receive what their faith and their works demand. Those who worked righteousness will receive the reward of the Lord. Those who have worked wrong will feel the wrath of the Lord.

2. The Two Appointments of God for Christ

As all people die once, so Christ died (and could only die) once. But whereas men and women die because they are sinners and are compelled to die, Christ died willingly, offering himself for sin. Now he is the Saviour of all who trust him to free them from the yoke of sin.

As judgment follows the death of each person, so judgment follows the death of Christ; except that he is not judged but is himself the Judge. That is how he will appear to many at his coming! But to those who are "eagerly looking for him" he will appear rather as Saviour.

When he comes the second time, his purpose will not be to deal with sin. Christ will not appear as a Man of Sorrows, coming to be made sin for others. On that day he will show himself as King over all, surrounded by the thundering praise of multitudes of angels. He appeared before in the likeness of sinful flesh; but then he will appear in the likeness of the glorious God.

He is coming to bring the fulfilment of all the hopes of his people, to cover the earth with the glory of the Lord, to redeem the entire creation from bondage, to clothe the redeemed with immortality and incorruptibility.

He is coming with salvation for those who are looking for him. By this, therefore, we may know who are the Lord's: they are those whose great hope and longing is for the second appearing of Christ. We learn also that the Lord requires us to be always waiting eagerly for his coming, constantly expecting his return.

May he find us looking upward when he comes!

CHAPTER THIRTEEN:

PRIEST

In our final passage from Hebrews, the apostle argues that the sacrifices of the old order were a failure, and he shows the finality of the new sacrifice made by God's true priest, Christ. He contrasts the two orders of priesthood, that of Aaron and that of Christ -

THE NEW SACRIFICE

- see Hebrews 10:1-10.

A. THE SHADOW SACRIFICES (vs 1)

The law - the old system of prescribed rules and ceremonies - was a mere "shadow" of the great things to come. Like a faint sketch, it was at best an imperfect representation of the ideal of God. It did have a useful purpose: it gave a meagre idea of the riches God was eager to lavish upon his people. By this enticing glimpse, the Lord planned to draw them eventually to the gospel. That is why he deliberately kept the law inadequate. He did not want them to become satisfied with it, and perhaps prefer it to Christ.

Moreover, the apostle declares that the law was not "the true form" of the good things God has promised. It fell short of the heavenly reality; it was only a "reflection". Thus he shows that the old form was

- not an exact likeness of the ideal sanctuary
- not a true image of the ideal priest
- not a full presentation of the ideal sacrifice
- not an actual conveyance of the ideal promise.

Know therefore, that the law of Moses - with its entire apparatus, all its provisions, ordinances, statutes - is nothing more than a grey shadow, a dim profile, of the gospel. It cannot make perfect those who adhere to it. Not all the keeping of its observances will add so much as a speck of holiness to any person.

How foolish then are Christians who strive to improve the perfections of Christ by keeping regulations about food, meat, drink, and days. Learn it:

"They can never bring to perfection anyone who tries by such things to draw near to God."

B. THE SUCCESSIVE SACRIFICES (vs 2)

When he speaks about the law in this passage, the apostle means the rules dealing with Israel's animal sacrifices. Those sacrifices were just "shadows" cast by the coming true Sacrifice. What value they had lay in this: they were reflections of Christ. Without him they lacked all validity. Like a silhouette, which provides a little joy during a time of separation, but will be quickly discarded when the beloved person returns, so were those shadowy offerings. A silhouette is precious because it resembles, though ever so slightly, the features of someone dear to you. An image of a stranger will not do. But who would prefer such a dim likeness to the warm and loving reality?

Sometimes you can see a shadow, but not the sun. Yet the shadow shows that the sun is in heaven and shining brightly. Eventually it will move across the sky and into your sight. You will then no longer be standing in darkness. So with Christ and the law. A new day has dawned. The beams of God are shining in another direction. The former shadows no longer exist. Christ himself, and Christ alone, stands as the One of whom the former things were but a misty outline.

The continual repetition of the old sacrifices shows their perpetual imperfection. Day by day, year by year, in a dreary succession of slaughter, a monotonous drudgery, the priests heaved onto the altar their holocausts. But that same endless reprise loudly declared their inadequacy. If the animal sacrifices had been effective in securing forgiveness of sin they would have ceased, further offerings being unnecessary.

Now here is a mark of an effective sacrifice: it will "purge the worshipper from all conscience of sin" (lit.). Notice -

1. Sacrifice is for Worshippers

No sacrifice, not even that of Christ, is effective in the life of any person who is not a "worshipper". Who is a worshipper? The word comes from a root that means "a hired menial", a servant of humble rank. At once we see the chief hindrance to someone becoming a true worshipper: pride. Humility is the first mark of a genuinely worshipful heart.

The word also means "to render homage", that is, to be diligent in the service of God. Humble service is God's rightful due. So let us give him all honour and reverence, offering our love, confessing our sin, lifting our voices in sincere prayer and praise. To all who walk this path of real worship the full benefits of Christ's sacrifice freely belong.

2. Sacrifice should "purge" sin

This the old sacrifices were unable to do. But those who present Christ as their sole sacrifice rest secure in the knowledge that

- they are purified from all iniquity
- the infection of sin is cleaned right away
- all that was unseemly has been broken
- the branches of the old nature have been pruned
- the guilt of sin is extinguished
- full reparation has been made for all unrighteousness.

This we must believe without wavering, who have fled to Christ for refuge. "Reckon yourselves to be truly dead to sin, but fully alive to God through Jesus Christ our Lord."

3. Sacrifice should purge the "conscience"

Here also the old oblations failed lamentably, but the once-for-all sacrifice of Jesus succeeded gloriously. The blood of Christ has startling power. Do you want freedom from every feeling of guilt, from all sense of short-coming, from all fear of failure, from all consciousness of sin? Then turn to the crucified One. His blood alone satisfies the restless cravings of conscience, which cannot find peace apart from real goodness. This the repetitive sacrifice of dumb beasts could never achieve.

C. THE SPURIOUS SACRIFICES (vs 3)

Daringly, the apostle brands the old sacrifices a pretence. How could they fulfil their promise to provide atonement for sin? How could they purge the worshipper's conscience? Did they not make sin more prominent by reminding the worshipper, year after year, that his iniquity was still with him? But the sacrifice of Christ, once embraced, fully absolves every sin. The cross at once places the believer in a state of righteousness. Nothing more is then required except to wash away daily defilement by repentance and faith in the Saviour.

The believer, looking back at Calvary, sees only that Christ has made full atonement for all sin. How impossible it was for the worshipper of old to find such satisfaction from his regular offerings! Each new Day of Atonement could only tell him that another sacrifice would be made the following year. Each new sacrifice could only remind him that he was still in a state of sin. Far from removing the consciousness of sin, those sacrifices constantly recalled the wrongdoing of the people and showed them their uncleanness before God.

D. THE SUPERFICIAL SACRIFICES (vs 4)

There was much that was foolish about those sacrifices of bulls and goats. Goats are objects of derision in common talk. The expression "make a goat of yourself" may be derived from the old Hebrew offering of a scapegoat (Le 16:8,10,26). As the priest led the trembling animal past them, the people often cried out against it. Seeing their own sins laid upon its head, they cursed the helpless victim.

Is this not a ludicrous spectacle? A grown man leading a terrified goat by a red ribbon, claiming that the sins of an entire nation could be carried away by it! The same could be said about Israel's other animal sacrifices, of bulls, sheep, and heifers. What worth can such brute beasts have, sufficient to undo the moral corruption of human beings?

Those animals were not of the same nature as humans; even less of the same nature as God. How powerless the blood of such sacrifices was to remove sin! How could these bleating creatures effect reconciliation between the people and God? They were but crude shadows of the one true Sacrifice, Christ.

E. THE SUPERFLUOUS SACRIFICES (vs 5-7)

The apostle quotes Ps 40:6-8 from the LXX, so it differs slightly from our present OT. Notice -

(1) The psalm predicts the words of the Son of God when he was born upon the earth. It is as though he asked the question, "Why have I been born?" Then, speaking by the eternal Spirit, he returns the answer -

> *"O God, thou hast neither desired nor delighted in burnt offerings. The sham of such sacrifices, shown by the continuing sin of the people, has made their altars*

disgraceful to thee. Thy desire has been for an obedient life, a consecrated spirit, a willing mind. Therefore thou hast provided me with a body, so that a perfect life and a perfect sacrifice may be offered unto thee."

(2) The unnecessary slaughter of countless beasts is an unpleasant spectacle. An ugliness lies in the wasted bodies of the scapegoats, the cries of pain from thousands of stricken sheep and cattle, the rivers of blood, the charred remains of the victims. People often accuse God of barbarity for installing such sacrifices. But now we see that God himself did not really want this wanton immolation. The massacred beasts, the burning flesh, grieved him. Such butchery brought no pleasure to the Lord

(3) Does this mean that the animal sacrifices were unnecessary? No, for it was better that brute beasts should die than a person made in the image of God. Yet in the end they were superfluous, for it says, "Sacrifices and offerings thou hast not desired." They brought no joy to heaven. Yet God himself commanded them? Yes, but not because he wanted them, only because the people needed them.

Even so, in Israel both before and after Moses set up his tabernacle, and also in the nations beyond Israel where no sacred altar was found, there was only one true remedy for sin. With or without a sacrifice, people who needed divine pardon had to come to God with fervent repentance and wholehearted trust. David's bitter confession in Psalm 51 provides a dramatic example of that principle. He knew too well that no goat could atone for his wickedness. Mercy must come to him from the grace of God alone, or salvation would escape him for ever.

(4) None of this was hidden in some back alley of scripture. "Turn to your own sacred writings," the apostle urged his Jewish readers, "and you will discover the futility of the old sacrifices." There also they would find several oracles that promised the inauguration of a new sacrifice. Here was an expiation that could not be prepared by the hand of a Jewish priest, but only by the hand of God.

One of those oracles tells how God's appointed Servant cried, *"A body hast thou prepared for me."* In the original psalm it reads, *"Mine ear hast thou pierced."*

Strange words! They allude to a custom described in Ex 21:1-6. Christ, speaking through the psalmist, likens himself to that Hebrew slave. Following the example of an ancient bondsman, Jesus loved God in whose service he laboured. He loved his bride the Church, given to him by God. He loved the children of that Church. He could not forsake them.

But notice a dramatic change that our text makes to the psalm. Only the ear of a Hebrew slave was stabbed and pinned to the door. But when the Holy Spirit applied the oracle to Jesus, he spoke about the "*body*" of Christ. Ah! such an infinity of suffering, such an immensity of love! When he made himself the Servant of God and the Saviour of mankind, Jesus yielded his *whole* body to the marring cross.

(5) The sacrifices of bulls and goats were prescribed by the levitical law. Therefore only the Aaronic priesthood could legally offer them. That is why it was essential for God's new priest (who was not of that priesthood) to offer a new sacrifice, outside that law. The new priest was Jesus, and the sacrifice was his body, which scripture says was "*prepared*" for him by God. So this was the final sacrifice, the only necessary sacrifice. It fully meets every demand of God and every need of men and women. It completes God's redemptive plan.

(6) Throughout his letter to the Hebrews the apostle argues for the supremacy of Christ. But this reference to Psalm 40 is probably his most conclusive proof. The Jews themselves widely saw that psalm as referring to the Messiah. Drawing on the words, "Lo, I have come," they named the Messiah, "He Who Comes," and they made this the foundation of their hope.

The apostle shows how Jesus fulfilled in every particular the requirements of scripture. Therefore he is the One who has come - his was the body prepared by God; his was the sacrifice accepted by God.

F. THE SECOND SACRIFICE (vs 8-9)

(1) Scripture says that God did not want the carcasses of bulls. Then it says, "But a body hast thou prepared for me." Thus the psalmist predicted a new sacrifice that would be acceptable to God, and that would bring him pleasure. So although the former sacrifices brought no joy to the Father, concerning this Man he says: "Behold my Servant, whom I uphold, my Chosen, in whom my soul delights!" (Is 42:1).

Therefore scripture rightly affirms: "He abolishes the first to establish the second."

We know then that the first was not satisfactory, because God abolished it. It was never truly pleasing to him. Therefore he annulled the law of the old altar. Whatever promise or power it may have had, God has now taken away. By the competent authority and irrevocable command of the King, that former law has been obliterated. It has no more authority over a Christian than the ancient laws of decayed empires have over present nations.

So Christ has removed the rule of the old law; only the record of it remains. Has it then no present use? Yes, for it reveals the method God used to bring men and women to Christ, and it assists us to grasp the meaning of Christ.

(2) Compulsion underlay the making of the old sacrifices: "they were offered according to the law." But the Second Sacrifice volunteered himself: "Lo, I have come to do thy will, O God." That promise, written so early into scripture, provided the way for people who lived before the coming of Christ to be sanctified. It guaranteed a coming payment that would secure their release from sin. On the ground of this foretold payment, God was willing to give eternal life to all who placed their faith in him, for he never doubted that the Son would make good all that he had spoken through the scriptures.

Christ himself made the same claim. He said, "I have come, just as the sacred scroll wrote about me." What he had promised through the Spirit, as recorded in scripture, he came to make good to the letter. He was as good as his word.

The OT presents in many places a portrayal of the future Saviour. Both in type and in clear statement, his coming was prophesied. For this reason, the old sacrifices had only one way to be effective. The people, on the basis of those prophecies, had to look past the blood of animals to that one perfect coming sacrifice. Only then did the former altar prevail over their guilt. The sacrifices then became a sign of faith in Christ, the mark of a willing heart, of a consecrated life. In that setting they were successful. But soon the priests began to slay animals merely as the price of purchasing pardon from God. Then the Lord despised their offerings and turned his face away from them (Is 1:11-15).

G. THE SUPERLATIVE SACRIFICE (vs 10)

In the Garden, Jesus said to his captors: "*If you seek me, let these other men go*" (Jn 18:8). What was the result? He was bound; his disciples escaped. But he was innocent, and they were guilty? Yes, but he was put to death, while they remained free.

What Jesus said then he still says to the Father: "*Let these people go free!*" If you are his disciple, then this is what he is saying to the Father about you. He says it because this is the will of God that he came to do.

Further, "*By that will we have been sanctified.*" It was the determined purpose of God to provide a means by which we could be sanctified; it was the willing choice of Christ to make himself that means; it was the voluntary sacrifice of Christ that effected the means; and the firm decree of God has established that means forever.

How rich is the grace of God! He could have fixed his will upon our destruction; instead he chose to fix it upon our deliverance!

Then he says, "*We have been sanctified through the offering of the body of Christ.*" Notice the past tense. The Cross has already achieved our full sanctification. What does that mean? To be sanctified is to be made holy. That is how God sees every person who comes into union with Christ by faith. It is not something we have to do; rather, nothing is required except to stand trustfully in the finished work of the Saviour.

You may doubt that your will is strong enough to bring you into holiness; but the will of God certainly is, and "*by that will you have been sanctified through the offering of the body of Christ*".

This is surely a cause for rejoicing. Yet it must also be a cause for reflection. If it is the will of God for us to be made holy, to be consecrated to him in Christ, then to live other than a holy life, to fail in that consecration, must violate the divine will and stir the anger of God. Does this mean that I must begin a sweaty struggle against sin, a struggle I am bound to lose? No! Let me rather yield with all my heart to the will of God, and allow him to carry me triumphantly into holiness!

To all who so love God, who earnestly desire to serve him, the glad promise comes: the offering of the body of Christ has made our sinful bodies holy. Consecration to Christ brings strength into flesh that was altogether weak; and whatever we still lack the superlative merits of Christ compensate for abundantly.

THE NEW PRIESTHOOD

- see He 10:11-18.

A. THE STANDING PRIESTS (vs 11)

Here is a striking mark of the *failure* of the old priesthood: God made no provision in the tabernacle for them to be seated. They had to stand while they ministered at the altar of the Lord.

Here is a striking mark of the *finality* of the second priesthood: before he began his intercessory ministry, Christ sat down at the Father's right hand (vs 12).

We shall consider this again in a moment, but notice first the purpose of sacrifice: "to take away sins." The word is different from that used in verse 4, and it *means "to remove completely ... to unveil ... to cast off anchor"*. The idea is that we were once thoroughly enveloped by sin; covered by it body, soul, and spirit; anchored to it, and unable to break free. Confronted by such total captivity the blood of bulls and goats remained helpless. But by the blood of Christ we can break loose from our sin. Now we can pull away from the shore of temptation, free ourselves from the sea-bed of our carnal nature, launch onto the ocean of righteousness, and sail away into holiness!

B. THE SEATED PRIEST (vs 12)

Those former priests stood in the holy place, which showed their subservience. This priest sits beside God, which shows his sovereignty.

Standing, they showed the incompleteness of their ministry. Sitting, he shows the finality of his.

The apostle drew the picture of Christ sitting at God's right hand from Ps 110:1 - "*The Lord says to my Lord, `Sit at my right hand until I turn your enemies into your footstool'*" (see also He 1:13; 5:6; 7:17,21; 8:1). This image then is no mere fancy, but a specific revelation of God, one that both Testaments link to the priestly ministry of the Messiah.

Jesus sat down because he had offered a single sacrifice, one sufficient to atone for all sin for all time. He *sat down*, satisfied that no person could ever sink so deep into sin that his sacrifice would be insufficient to redeem them. He sat down, and now, glorified at the right hand of the Majesty on high, he calmly awaits the subjugation of all his enemies. Therefore we see him as

C. THE SERENE PRIEST (vs 13)

"Then to wait" says one translation, which is a rather tame rendering of the more dynamic Greek, *"henceforth expecting"*. He is not merely waiting; he is expecting. It is a stance of faith. He triumphs because he believes. He rests content in his finished work, knowing that his death and resurrection have laid the immovable foundations of victory.

What characterises him, (*"sitting and expecting"*) should characterise us, if we believe in him. How could there now be room in us for anxiety? How could we doubt that we shall reach the chosen goal? Surely you can no longer question that Satan will be trodden down and that we shall inherit the kingdom prepared for us from the beginning! So Christ, sitting serenely in the heavens, is setting us an example of untroubled trust, and he rightly commands us to follow it. Just because he is sitting and expecting we know that the outcome is certain. The same rule applies to our walk of faith. What Christ died to gain for us will unfailingly come to those who hold serenely to the promise.

Just as our faith is the victory that overcomes the world (1 Jn 5:4), so this too is the victory of the Son of God: even his faith. Henceforth he *expects* that every enemy, demon and human, will be crushed. Beneath the onslaught of that relentless expectation, the ramparts of hell are crumbling stone by stone. As the soft water rolls against the rocky shore in endless search for the passage it will eventually wear for itself, so the impact of that silent hope of Christ, battering down the ramparts of darkness, fills the hosts of hell with despair.

D. THE SANCTIFYING PRIEST (vs 14)

Christians are people whom the one offering of Christ has sanctified. That is, despite any fault that may still be in them, they are for Christ's sake reckoned to be holy by God. We have already seen something of what this means. But now the writer adds a new dimension to it.

A troubling thought has occurred to him.

Perhaps his readers will suppose that because they always have to rest upon the reckoning of God, they will never arrive at real holiness? So he hastens to assure them that God's goal is actual perfection.

The offering of Christ holds limitless merit and power. Therefore it ensures final perfection for all who believe in him. This is a perfection gained, not by their working, but by his grace. Yet it will nonetheless be real. They will be perfect. Truly free from every infirmity, from every blemish, they will at last know the endless joy of holiness. The blood of Christ will keep them free even from the possibility of falling again into corruption, for he has "perfected for all time" those whom he has sanctified.

What certainty is ours! We know ourselves now to be sanctified, and to be advancing toward perfection. This beauty will be wrought in us infallibly (unless we forsake Christ), for there is nothing temporary about the work of Christ. What he has done he has done well, and done permanently.

This work, of course, cannot find its consummation until the day of resurrection. But meanwhile we see in the daily victories we now gain, and in our growth toward maturity in Christ, a foretaste of that blessed and happy hour of celebration.

E. THE SIGNIFIED PRIEST (vs 15)

The Holy Spirit has provided evidence. He is the True Witness of the amazing ability of Christ to take a sinful human life and, by the sole agency of his one offering of himself, to sanctify it wholly. This witness stirs within every believer when the Spirit tells them they are children of God (Ro 8:16-17). But mostly it is found in scripture; so the apostle quotes Jeremiah (31:33-34). He has quoted this passage before (He 8:10-12), where his emphasis was on the idea of a new covenant. Here he emphasises the idea that God will never again remember our sin -

F. THE SAVIOUR PRIEST (vs 16-17)

Having promised to make a new covenant with his people, God then says: "Never again will I remember their sins or their iniquities."

In the original text the word "remember" means either "to be fixed in the mind", or "to reward or punish". The latter sense is the one intended here. God cannot banish all actual recollection of sin from his mind, for he cannot with integrity re-write history. But he can judicially forget sin. That is, he can strike it from the records of the heavenly court, so that no charges are listed against us.

In other words, sin may be remembered as a fact, but it is no longer remembered as a criminal offence, for Christ has satisfied all the demands of the law. The blood of Jesus washes all guilt from the believer. The thing most firmly fixed in the Father's mind is no longer my sin, but the righteousness of Christ.

This seems too incredible! Can it be true that the Father no longer recalls my sin, that he is not obliged to exact a penalty from me, that my sin is forgotten? Yes, because he says plainly, "I will not remember your iniquity!" It is too good for me! Yes, but not too good for Christ! God might refuse me, but he cannot refuse Jesus; and for his sake God makes the unequivocal promise, "Your sins will remain forever forgotten!"

G. THE SUPERIOR PRIEST (vs 18)

If you read the Letter to the Hebrews, you will notice that this verse marks the end of the doctrinal section of the letter. Then, with verse 19, the apostle begins to apply his doctrine. He shows the Christians how to make use of the great truths he has shared with them. So verse 18 is the climax to his argument, the final outcome of his sweeping claims about the superiority of Jesus. It all results in this: there will never be any other offering for sin.

The forgiveness wrought at Calvary was so comprehensive, so final, that all other ways of approaching God were at once demolished. Nothing remains now except for the sinner to repent, to believe in Jesus, and then to begin working out this immense salvation in daily life.

CHAPTER FOURTEEN:

SUMMARY SO FAR

CLIMAX

All that I have written above is actually a preparation for the marvellous theme that will occupy my next book: The Royal Priesthood of the Believer. But I want to bring this study to an end by summarising what we have so far discovered about the consequences of the ascension of Christ -

(1) The Holy Spirit was Given

"Jesus was raised from the dead by God, of which we are all witnesses. He is now exalted at God's right hand, and having received from the Father the promised Holy Spirit, he has richly bestowed this gift, which you can see and hear" (Ac 2:33).

(2) The Church is Established

The continued existence of the church depends upon the ascension; for while Christ "sits" in heaven, nothing can destroy it!

(3) Christ's Eternal Priesthood is Established

There is a remarkable story in John 20:11-18. On the morning of Jesus' resurrection Mary met him near the empty tomb. She at first mistook him for a gardener, but recognised him as soon as he spoke her name. Her immediate instinct was to cling to him in rapturous re-union, as though never to part from him again. But he withdrew from her, saying,

"Do not cling to me. I have not yet ascended to the Father."

He meant that she would lose him for ever, not gain him, if he did not first ascend back to his Father. But the ascension confirms his promise, "I will surely be with you always, even to the very end of time!" (Mt 28:20) Consequently, he now calls his disciples, not friends, but "brothers", which is a mark of his astonishing love. Notice, however, that this is his grace, not our familiarity; the apostles did not presume to call him "brother". He may call us his friends; we call him Lord. Jesus himself made this distinction when he used the strange expression, "I am ascending to my Father and to your Father, to my God and to your God." Our relationship to God and the Father differs from his. God is Father to Christ in a mystery that is exalted far above our understanding. Nevertheless, though he sits at the Father's right hand, because of the ascension he is able to call himself our "brother", and delights to deal with us in love.

But there is a deeper dimension to his refusal to allow Mary to hold him before he had returned to the Father. The law of Moses in Le 16:15-17, 23-26 forbade anyone to touch the high priest from the moment he began to sprinkle the blood on the great Day of Atonement until after he had fully cleansed the sanctuary and the people. In between, he had to enter the innermost part of the tabernacle and splash the blood on the "mercy seat" - the golden lid of the Ark of the Covenant. In fulfilment of the ancient type, Jesus had to enter the heavenlies and present to the Father the evidence that he had made full atonement for all sin. Only after that could he show himself again to his disciples and allow them to touch him.

So his encounter with Mary in the garden was the first step in his assumption of the heavenly high priesthood, and it marked the beginning of the new relationship that was being established between heaven and earth.

(4) His Intercessory Ministry is Established

The word "intercede" is based on two Latin words that mean "a go-between"; thus Christ ever stands between us and God, pleading our cause before the Father, obliging the Father, as it were, to see us only through him. With such an Advocate how can our plea at heaven's bar fail?

(5) The Ascension Gifts have been Given

These heavenly gifts are found in two kinds: the ministry gifts of Christ (Ep 4:11-14); and the charismatic gifts of the Spirit (1 Co 12:7-11)

Where these gifts are denied, the ascension of Christ is likely to become theoretical rather than powerful; where the ascension is strongly perceived, these gifts are likely to flourish.

(6) We are Made Royal Priests in Christ

For us, this is the highest consequence of the ascension of Christ, and it represents perhaps the most exciting theme in Christian theology. However, its study will have to occupy another book.

Let me conclude this one with a passage from the Puritan divine, Thomas Watson (died 1690) -

> "How the scene is altered! When he was on earth, he lay in a manger; now he sits on a throne. Then he was hated and scorned of men; now `God hath given him a name above every name.' Then he came in the form of a servant, and as a servant stood with basin and towel, and washed his disciples' feet; now he is clad in his prince's robes, and the kings of the earth cast their crowns before him. On earth he was a man of sorrow; now he is anointed with the oil of gladness. On earth was his crucifixion; now his coronation. Then his Father frowned upon him in desertion; now he has set him at his right hand. Before he seemed to have no form of beauty in him; now he is the brightness of his Father's glory. Oh, what a change is here! `Him hath God highly exalted!'"

BIBLIOGRAPHY

Believer's Bible Commentary; William Macdonald; Thomas Nelson Publishers; 1989.

Bible Background Commentary; Intervarsity Press, Nottingham UK; 1993.

Bible Knowledge Commentary, The; by John Walvoord and Roy Zuck; Cook Communications, Colorado Springs, Colorado; 1989.

Calvin's Commentaries; John Calvin (1509-1564).

Christian Classics; ed. Veronica Zundel; Eerdmans Pub. Co., 1983.

College Press NIV Commentary, The; Joplin, Missouri; 1996.

Commentary on Ephesians, A; Charles Hodge (1797-1878).

Commentary on the Bible; Adam Clarke (1715-1832).

Commentary On The Old And New Testaments, A; John Trapp (1601-1669).

Commentary on the Old and New Testaments, A; Robert Jamieson, A. R. Fausset, David Brown; 1871.

Explanatory Notes on the Whole Bible; John Wesley (1703-1791).

Exposition of the Entire Bible; John Gill (1690-1771).

Expositor's Bible Commentary, The; ed. Frank E. Gaebelein; Zondervan Publishers, Grand Rapids, Michigan.

Expository Commentary; H.A. Ironside (1876-1951).

Holman New Testament Commentary; ed. Max Anders; B & H Publishing Group, Nashville, Tennessee; 2004.

Interpreter's Bible, The; Abingdon Press, New York; 1952.

IVP New Testament Commentary Series, The; Intervarsity Press, Nottingham, UK.

Jewish New Testament Commentary; David H. Stern; Jewish New Testament Publications, Inc., Clarksville, Maryland; 1982.

Matthew Henry's Commentary; Marshall, Morgan, and Scott, London; 1953.

Matthew Poole's Commentary; 1685

Nelson's New Illustrated Bible Commentary; Thomas Nelson Inc., New York; 1999.

New Testament Commentary; Baker's Publishing House, Grand Rapids, Michigan; 1987.

Notes on the Bible; Albert Barnes (1798-1870).

People's New Testament Commentary, The; B. W. Johnson; Word Search Corporation, Nashville, Tennessee; 2010.

People's New Testament, The; by B. W. Johnson; 1891.

Poor Man's Commentary On The Whole Bible, The; Robert Hawker; 1850.

Preacher's Commentary, The; Word Inc., Nashville, Tennessee; 1992.

Preacher's Outline and Sermon Bible; Word Search Corporation, Nashville, Tennessee; 2010.

Pulpit Commentary, The; ed. Joseph S. Exell, Henry Donald Maurice Spence-Jones; 1881.

Vincent's Word Studies; Marvin R. Vincent; 1886

Wiersbe's Expository Outlines; Warren W. Wiersbe; Publisher, David C. Cook, Colorado Springs, Colorado.

Word Pictures In The New Testament; A. T. Robertson; 1933.

www.ingramcontent.com/pod-product-compliance
Lightning Source LLC
Chambersburg PA
CBHW052008090426
42741CB00008B/1600